Can't Stop Crying - Rise!

RIZE LAMONT MCGILL

ISBN: 978-1-5356-0823-7

TABLE OF CONTENTS

CHAPTER ONE

Rise

The minute I put myself in a room alone, the fire of a gun went off in my mind. I broke into tears. I realized that the gun misfired and I was saved. I broke into tears and rediscovered my hero powers were called upon by God. Right there and then, I knew my mission. He guided me to create illustrations and animate characters that I have never done before and to use all the years of a quarter of a century of working with young people as a teacher and counselor with huge success and to apply my God-given gifts of understanding the hearts of people and let it be known how they are feeling.

After three years of completing my animated characters out of an apple, everything in me came to a halt. I couldn't move. God told me to go on the internet to see for myself. I saw the most disturbing distressful video of a child of God walking home from school and two unsuspecting friends come from behind a trailer and some bushes and punched the child and pulled the child's hair. She had her head up to God with her arms folded across her backpack as if she was already praying that she make it home. Then another child beating on a child and another child keeping a diary and timeline of her death with scars to indicate weeks of planning. There was more than I could stand! The imprint had gone straight through the depths of me. I never felt helpless like that ever before in my life.

I went online to reach out to all that I could. I could not rest; I could not stop crying! Day after day, hour after hour, and minute by minute, until I could be heard. No child should ever be ignored at this level and for our nation to focus on Walls and Emails leads me to toss my rock into the river to reach the ripples of the hearts of people.

I have taught as a schoolteacher and worked as a counselor for young people for over a quarter of a century! My engagement: I have met with several doctors and they all say I have an enlarged heart! My response is, "How did you know? I'm from Philly, and just like in Philadelphia, cities, towns, there is a lot of violence, shootings, and gang banging! I know you are angry and I am too! You know what, give that anger to God.

I kept my focus and so can you! Everybody has a gift from God! So do you! If you don't know what it is, that makes you talented with natural abilities, ask a friend, ask a relative or a neighbor! Once you discover your gift, allow that gift to guide you into success. See the world. Perfect!" There are a ton of people that care; they are all around like on Facebook and school professionals as well as counselors at your service. I am on Facebook and I have a website filled with love and support for you. Get dialed in… By the way, my gift is understanding the hearts of people. Here's how!

*   *   *   *

Growing up in the hood in Philadelphia, Pennsylvania and being raised by my mother who was a single parent with five children, and several boyfriends along the way, she kept us safe with food and shelter most of the time. She loved to laugh and taught us to be unselfish. She gave us all chores, got us ready for church and made sure we spent time with relatives. She taught us to beware of "Stranger Danger" by reminding us to walk to stores, school, or go out to play within sight of each other.

Her loving heart was infectious and she loved to laugh and could find the humorous side of most things. She was warm and affectionate and considered to be fun to interact with.My oldest brother had babysitting duties and would not hesitate to keep us in line if we did not follow directions that our mother told us. Ordered by a slap upside the head or a promise that it would happen if limits were over the top.

He was the innovator of the home and his gift was being the first to play the instrument, such as the guitar, in the family. He was proof that practice and determination could make a difference if you never gave up.

He earned a spot as a professional guitar player for multiple gospel groups. My other two brothers are twins. The older of the two had been the most energetic. He had a loving heart.

He was very passionate about how life is supposed to be and the understanding why things go wrong. He made time to explain, guide, and share his views and encourage the family to not let the problems make us feel bad. His gift is holding the same job for over 30 years! He demonstrated empathy. His younger twin is the professor. He had always been the most curious in the family. If something did not look or feel right, he had to know why. He had to know what make things work and if it did not he wanted to fix it. He has a loving heart and carries his closeness to God everywhere he goes.

My sister is loving and doesn't hesitate to engage her discoveries about life to show the beauty of all living things. She encouraged the family to think before reacting. She had always been an explorer and cared deeply for me and made every moment educational. She was the protector like our mother and wanted the best of life to be our guide and avoid the unattractive side of things such as people with bad energy that caused people to be aggressive.

As for me, the youngest, I have always been a peacemaker. I always found the beautiful side of the people I meet and like to let it be known to them. Being kind and enjoying life; helping others and keeping God in my heart. I'm described as friendly, humble, easy going, and like surrounding myself with positive people. Here's how I grew up:

Philadelphia, Pennsylvania, otherwise known affectionately as "Philly," is historically the birthplace of independence for our country. The Declaration of Independence was written in Philadelphia and it has been known as the place of "brotherly love." People do have a level of issues and problems like any place on earth but the difference is how it is settled and ways to model excellence for solving problems like no other place. Kindness, courtesy, and the demand for respect or put up your fists to settle it like men!

Afterwards, handshakes hugs and lifelong friendships are the result! "Like brothers!" As for girls, they actually did have rules of fighting and followed the code of no pulling of the hair! I don't condone fighting; it's just a fact of life. As a counselor, you will discover your hero powers, spiritual guidance, and path of your gifts from God, ways to find support, coping skills, social skills, positive decision making skills, and the like of many secrets to become a peaceful, assertive, productive and responsible citizen too!

The food in Philadelphia taste fantastic! Full of rich traditions, culture, religion, sports, and music, the loving atmosphere is second to none! A place of pride and, in spite of camaraderie, there is the spirit of competition. Most everyone wears a garment with a sports team with the name *Philadelphia* written on it someplace. If a neighbor, or family, or someone had a problem with their car or a woman is in distress, you better believe a Philadelphian or two will happily come to your rescue! If you leave Philadelphia for pursuit of a career or a better life, the love and spirit of Philadelphia forever stays in your heart!

Philadelphia is the birthplace of independence for land, peace, freedom, and filled with God-fearing families. Where else should the pursuit of kindness spread?

Many traditions that I grew up with still remain in my heart. My mother grew up in Lumberton, North Carolina. She moved to Philadelphia at a young age. She was in search for a better life and a better way of living. Her values and morals made her who she is and attending church like she did growing up carried on and like generations before her as church runs deep! She had us kids go every Sunday and no was not an option unless you wanted a spanking on the backside and crying on the way to church service!

Settling in on North Philadelphia, our family attended church every Sunday. My pastor, Bishop McCloud at Holy Bible Church of Lord and Christ, kept me deeply rooted in religion and taught me to keep God in my heart. With church in our heart and my oldest brother's guitar skills, my mother put the family together to form a gospel singing group. My twin brother, two of my cousins, and myself sang gospel! We had a powerful message and churches that had us sing felt not only the pastor's message from preaching but also spiritual gospel up lifting!

I was the youngest of the group and the youngest would get a lot of attention, especially at age five. My brothers made me pay later with slaps across the head to keep my ego in check. We did sound amazing. We had a toe-tapping, knee-slapping, get-up-on-your-feet popping reaction from the church! Shouting, spiritual uplifting, fire and brimstone reactions that church members would not forget!

Our mother, church members, and the pastor were all very proud of us. We made our church proud and it made me feel proud to be part of it! I never forgot the lyrics years later. Soon after much success and happiness of living in one section of North Philadelphia, our family moved away and the Gospel group departed. What was the purpose for so many moves?

There's violence, gangs, shootings, robberies and it was like that every time we moved someplace else. So why so often and for what reason did we move a lot? I could bore you, but as a former teacher, I would like to tell you in the form of a story and how I discovered my gifts from God.

In the Bible: 2 Timothy 3

"Remember that there will be difficult times in the last days. 2. People will be selfish, greedy, boastful, and conceited; they will be insulting, disobedient to their parents, ungrateful and irreligious; 3 they will be unkind, merciless, slanderers, violent, and fierce; they will hate the good; 4 they will be treacherous, reckless, and swollen with pride; they will love pleasure than God; 5 they will hold to the outward from of our religion, but reject its real power. Keep away from such people."

The king is experiencing great concern for his beautiful queen. To keep his queen's failing heart filled with continuous spiritual energy, love, and kindness, he went to her bedside to share a story that describes the essences of the Land of Reason, which is kindness and how they fell in love! A man came upon a child struggling to carry a bag of apples, he unhorsed himself, put the bag of apples on his horse as one of the apples fell to the ground and rolled away, and he put the child on the horse and gave the child a ride to town.

The child was grateful, thanked the man, and noticed an old lady appearing hungry and gave her fruit from his fruit stand. The old lady thanked the little owner of the fruit stand headed home to make apple pie. On her way home, she alertly noticed a child dashing across the rode unaware of racing horses and saved her life as she caught her before the horses could run her over. The mother of the child thanked the old lady and gave her a valuable stone.

The old lady used her valuable stone to help her grandson make toys out of wood for children to play and share in a play area safely. The play area became as source to teach children ways to be careful and it made the town proud. The town elected a teacher the watch over the children. The teacher came to thank the grandson for his toy making skills. The grandson became a king and married the teacher.

CHAPTER TWO

The queen's attempt to smile upon their romantic courtship: that is a story also told over and again by the people in the Land of Reason, which had little effect, the King finished his story and the queen was no more! She fell into a deep sleep and couldn't open her eyes. King Dontavius became alarmed! He called on his son!

Rise, you carry the gift of kindness and the understanding of the hearts of others that are desperately needed in the new land named, Earth! You are required to go create a movement to represent your spirit. For world order, find the child they call 'Coodie.' Protect him with all you have. He will receive the spirit! Just like deception here, there will be deception there. Without evil they will not receive kindness. I must stay and look after my queen.

Her heart aches for world order here and the place called Earth. There is bad news! Your sister was taken several hours ago. This is the evil I speak of. We believe she was taken to a church and put to sleep. My eyes do not work like they used to anymore. The boy, Coodie, will lead you to your sister and be careful because the evil has great power. Coodie has a big heart! He should be easy to find. His mother is protecting him and needs help. He draws attention for his kindness and good will. Positive energy is real. Go! Go now! Remember the evil's magical power ain't got nothing against your spiritual power! Just believe! I will, old man! Said Rise!

Earth is not the same since war 700 years ago! Most everything else is the same except there have never been enough honey and biscuits around! A new offspring has emerged and as history repeats itself, another destruction is on its way again! Only this time, there may be one chance of hope. One opportunity to be heard; one child with enough kindness in his heart that dares to be a prince for peace. His name is Coodie the Bear. In fact, the entire planet is run by this breed. Quite a name for a cub but fitting for his character. Coodie is very cute, with charm, wit, and influence because he speaks from the heart. It is not his exterior that is cute—even though some may disagree— it is his infinity for kindness and his ability to understand the hearts of people by way of kindness! Coodie is a peace maker and in spite of his rough upbringing, Coodie will sacrifice his life for the sake of peace! Real talk!

There are many rumors that follow Coodie such as the ability to see by design like time, space, and matter, like how an engine works in an automobile without opening the hood of a car ever! And other rumors like connecting to the minds and predicting the future, or simply his intelligence or being super smart, all of which may be true but one thing is for sure, he does have a big heart! Here's what I mean by many of his stories.

At the dead of winter with visibility on the roads were down to a minimal at best and because of a loose wiper blade that did not help very much, Coodie's family of five were at a traffic stop with the family asleep except for anxious Coodie because in five minutes, Coodie would be turning 12 years old. "Just five more minutes, Mom!" says Coodie. Before he turns his head to check if his mother is listening, she is looking at the rearview mirror religiously! "Mom, did you hear me?"

"Yes boy, hush!" Coodie knows she did not hear him because this isn't an answer he had heard before but when she is worried, distracted or when listening to "grown folks talking!" Coodie has pretty good instincts so he decides to check his mother's thinking. "I see 'em on my side, Mom!"

"Who? The agents!"

"What agents, Mom!? What are you so nervous about?" says Coodie.

"Nothing! Stop scaring me like dat!"

When a mother says, "Stop scaring me like dat," there are more reasons to be scared. The family had been moving every two to three years since Coodie could remember! Coodie's birthday became less important and the focus shifted from Coodie's birthday to the big word: "Fear."

Coodie's mother was hiding the family and running away like clockwork to keep the family safe. From what and from whom? There were no signs that Coodie had been aware of and Coodie haven't noticed any suspicious behavior. Coodie began to check the mirror himself. No special agents from any cartoons he had ever seen, like the black cars with men wearing glasses and seem to always be looking straight ahead then turn their car when spotted! Nothing like that! So why be so paranoid and secretive? I could tell you why, but I would need to shoot you with a ray gun! Just kidding. My most educated guess begins in this manner, and remember, it's an educated guess.

At just six months old, Coodie's mother and father were sitting in the kitchen feeding Coodie. The radio was playing and Coodie's mother (who loved to laugh) and father sat at the kitchen table telling stories as little Coodie joined in on the fun. After all, laughing releases positive energy and Coodie thrived on the opportunity even at just six months of age. Coodie laughed at each punch line right on cue. They easily laughed about every six seconds!

Coodie's father stopped to stare at Coodie because he laughed with his parents! Suddenly, Coodie's father made a face of fascination and said, "Coodie, can you understand the words that are coming out of Daddy's mouth?"

Coodie smiled and said, "Da Da!"

"See look he knows!"

"Let me ask him," Coodie's mother said, "what's my name cutie?" (Coodie's name changed to "Cute-tee" when his mother was proud of something Coodie did and it was her way of letting him know it.)

"Ma ma!"

They looked at each other as if they had seen a UFO! Coodie's mother went to turn the radio down and asked Coodie again, "What's my name?"

"Da Da and Ma Ma!"

They both were so astounded, they nearly fell back out of their seats! Dad ran out of the room! It frightened little Coodie but he chilled! After all, Coodie enjoyed the company and his favorite honey and biscuits!

They ran back into the room where Coodie was and the energy was super and by this time they brought back a couple of friends with them. Coodie's mother handed him another biscuit and bounced back as if his baby chair had electricity coming off it! Mother said, "Say my name, Cutie!"

"Ma Ma and Da Da!"

They broke out in a huge laugh, and still astounded by the discovery. They went to get more friends and asked again. The fourth time, Coodie began to wonder if his parents knew their own name. Coodie began to get confused and told himself, "If my parents don't know their name maybe I'm too young to tell them." Coodie shut down and waited until he was sure and stuck to baby talk soon after!

How did Coodie have a gift of comprehension at such an early age? Were his superpowers on all the time? Did his parents know their names? And where were his brothers and sister? Finally, at birth, did a mad scientist or secret agent sneak a wonder pill in Coodie's parents' drink while dining out? Well I could tell you but you gotta hold your breath for ten seconds first. One, two, three, four… just kidding!

Breathe please! Good job! Pass me a drink, I'm thirsty too… thanks! Check out this superpower:

Coodie was just three years old. He loved to laugh just like his mother, and loudly! He was invited to a party. Most of the cubbies were older than him and his fear was being left alone at a party. Yes, people leave others alone at parties. That's not fun, right? Nobody should feel lonely at a party. Agreed! Oddly enough, Coodie's siblings were not there again! The party had older bears there. Hmm, now that is a mystery!

Coodie's superpowers began to kick in and his ability of telekinesis (the ability to make things move) wasn't working. Coodie tried wiggling his two fingers, the head nod in his direction, and lastly, "You will stay here in this room!" inside his mind. Finally, Coodie tried saying something with sound effects like a cool whistle or dropping a drink on the ground.

Well the spill worked for all of ten seconds to clean up. "Thank you," Coodie said to the older crowd of apple bears and nothing he said could keep them interested enough to spend time with him. Rejected! In fact, each sentence without him began pushing them toward the kitchen like a magnet was tugging them away! And it happened. One of the older apple bears that were much taller and slicker said, "Why don't we go into the other room so the little bears can play in here?"

Coodie needed to admit: he was a smooth talker too, because there were just two boys and four girls. One of the girls said, "Okay!" and Coodie nearly cried. He did not give up. His fear was too great! Not that his peers were fun, Coodie liked hearing how older bears got along. His superpowers kicked in again. Little Coodie came up with an idea from his imagination (that part of the brain where one can put pictures into images and images into ideas!)

Chapter Three

While watching the movement that was generated by the "smooth talker," Coodie tried to be a step ahead but it was nearly too late because the words that had been spoken nearly crushed him! "Coodie was crushed but still he kept his cool! His hero-imagination antenna was not high enough so he adjusted it and *boom*! It hit him! Little Coodie said, "Hey if we play a game can I stay with you and talk?"

"Okay," said the slick-and-pretend-to-care bear! "Tell us what game?"

Coodie said, "Take this party cup and hide it anywhere in the kitchen and I will tell you where it is."

They began to get excited. "What, little bear?"

Coodie let out a little pee. Thank goodness nobody saw it but a grin did came from behind him! Coodie said, "If I win, I can hang out with ya'll right?"

Coodie had no idea what he was doing but if his mind could imagine, the idea might just follow! Coodie made sure to make eye contact at the smooth-talking leader—he was clearly in charge. The smooth talker, "Sweet as honey, show us money! What-cha working with!" Which meant, "Okay you can hang out with us."

Little did they know, Coodie was thrilled but was also waiting for his superpowers to kick in and going to bathroom did enter his mind. Coodie had honey, biscuits, and milk. Milk on an empty stomach is a little annoying, even for bears! The smooth talker was too smooth because he left out the other three- and four-year olds. Coodie whispered, "Come with us!"

One said, "That's okay."

Others, one four-year old said, "We are just fine."

Funny thing: his words did not match his age said, "its okay go ahead and show them the trick!"

Coodie looked angry! It's said that one person's short term pleasure will inevitably lead to long-term pain. Having faith is a good thing though! Believing in yourself is a better thing or equal! Coodie went into the kitchen to have a look around. Everyone was tickled by the thought of seeing by design.

They were so happy and excited that Coodie nearly forgot he was the main meal of the picnic basket. Coodie told them to hide the cup anywhere in the kitchen. It was about to go down! Coodie's powers kicked in. The answer was guessing at best!

Just kidding. I know you believe more and more you shall know. The approach is thought versus thinking! Sounds the same, but the application is different.

I know one is present and the other is past tense, but work with me. Actually, there is a difference when both words apply. For example, what you thought is different from what the group is thinking, therefore, think like them!

The excitement and energy became an all-time high! And Coodie still needed to use the restroom! "Okay, leave the room!" they said at the same time.

Coodie took another look before he left the room. "Well, leave the room!" one of the pretty girl bears said, "Go, Cutie," with a big grin and turned little Coodie by the shoulder and walked him past the hanging beads that separated the room a from the kitchen. The image was a refrigerator, clubbers everywhere, drawers, a table, more cabinets, and another table with containers on top, and a place to store pots below.

"Okay, come in!" yelled the cubs. The excitement was too much to handle and the girl cubs began to squeal! Not like a pig but like they are straining to poo! Now transforming into holding pom-poms and on the tip of their toes, " Where is it?" said the smooth talker with an impatient tone of voice.

Coodie enjoyed the attention from the girl bears and Mr. "Where is it!" kill-joy interrupted a perfect connection!

"I got-cha'll, didn't I?" Coodie had a favorite saying during a moment of heightened excitement that contained 1,000 question marks behind it. It is a combination of the words "gotcha" and "ya'll" together. Coodie's reaction to a room of kindness! One can always discover their gift in unsuspecting ways and it can be found in speech, actions, and in cases of emergencies! Try it yourself.

Ready, two bears came to a water fountain for a drink of water at the same time. One says, "Go ahead, you first!" What is his or her superpower? If you said kindness, then you are right! If you said politeness, you are also right. Being polite is just like kindness in many ways! Good job! For big bears, kindness is allowing other drivers to pass or for pedestrian-bears to cross the street.

Imagine a world where the horn of a car is only used to warn and not complain. Big Apple bears model for little bears and living a peaceful way adds years to your life. Deep breathing is a great way to just take it easy. It's the little things in kindness that make the world go round! "I love you!" Now back to Coodie's cup guessing activity!

"Sure, little bear, prove it!" said Mr. Smooth Talker! They hid the cup five times and Coodie got it right each time by naming the location of the cup! Two of the five times, they hid the cup in another room! Coodie thought that was unfair. He already imagined whose idea it was to put the cup in another room. (Mr. Johnny-Smooth!)

When the time came for Coodie's mother to pick him up, the parents from the party began to whisper to Coodie's mother about his superpowers from the "cup activity." Coodie's mother gave him a long stare! Was Coodie in trouble? *Pop*! "Ouch!" said Coodie, "What was that for?" It was the four-year-old that refused to participate in the activity. He turned his head back again to give a dirty look and two long stares and said, "I got my eye on you, Coodie."

Coodie's mother got into the car and took off in a rush. "Did you hear about the party and all the fun I had?"

Coodie's mother did not answer. A rare occurrence just occurred.

"Did I do something wrong?"

Coodie's mother appeared alarmed and full of focus with her eyes on the road ahead.

"No everything is fine. Did you have fun?"

The fun bubble just popped! Could this be the incident that caused Coodie's family to move? Coodie struggled with his mother's decision to move again and still could not understand why. He imagined the party went well.

Imagine matching the interest by looking from the eyes of your friend and building on what makes them happy—just kindness through inclusion. If for some reason, your superpowers are not on yet, tell a story that made you laugh, hand out a treat to others, sincere compliments, share likes about others only, current events that are fun, and ignore negative comments that are shared in groups by simply saying, "Excuse me, I'm thirsty; would you like something?" When you return, the conversation will be over and if not it's your out to interact with others that are positive! Taaadaaaaahhhh!

The silent ride home was louder than words on the way home that evening of the party. Coodie could hear the sounds of the wheels struggling to grip the snow-ridden streets. The homes and houses were made of logs and beaver-glue, which was broken leaves, weeds, debris, sticks, branches, and rocks. The roads are made of leaves, soil, and broken sticks that covered old man-made roads from centuries ago.

CHAPTER FOUR

The remnants of houses and homes that stood in pieces were historic reminders of what not to do as the corners and broken doorways maintained its broken structure. The day was nearly over and the reflections of the sunlight appearing like dancing angles flickering onto the broken stained gate of glass windows from ancient churches stimulated rods of Coodie's pupils. Coodie's wide eyes responded like receptors while his mother glanced at him.

The dance played on his pupils in slow motion like an old movie projector turning pages of scriptures from a bible. Coodie received the Holy Ghost! Coodie asked with his eyes fixed on the screen, "Mom what do the colorful windows mean on the churches?"

Coodie's mother said, "God!"

"God put colors on churches?" he asked.

"No Cutie, they show that they are churches and different religions all have them on their window."

"They are very pretty!" said Coodie. "Mom there was something about religion I don't understand but I got it!"

There was more to his words that wintery evening while riding in the passenger seat with his mother driving because it was Christmas Eve! Coodie's mother smiled at him with wide eyes! After the blessing that Coodie received from the scriptures of reflection, he arose with spiritual energy.

Coodie's mother glanced at him a little more than usual while driving home that Christmas night. For the first time, her spirit had been renewed after hearing, "…something about religion I just don't understand, but I got it!"

She felt reassured that God smiled on her son and no longer feeling weather or not it was magical powers but spiritual powers upon her son! All of the multiple experiences questioned her faith about her son's behavior. After all, whomever enters a person's life may neither have the best heart, spiritual, nor best intentions in mind. People fear what they don't understand. However, her spiritual confidence became short lived. Just when his mother was about to share a thought to form a gospel group with Coodie and his family members, a screeching meteor entered Earth's atmosphere at the same time! "What is dat?"

"All systems go!" said Juan-Tracy! Rize's eyes, otherwise known as his navigator! Juan-Tracy was from the same place Rize was from: the Place of Reason! Juan-Tracy met Rize while he was training for his purpose. Rize's sister, Kahlia, and JuanTracy were fans. Juan-Tracy had an amazing connection with all the animals and birds. Juan-Tracy could not speak but his other senses were heightened and are gifts from God! Juan-Tracy spoke, but nothing came out of his mouth. One day while JuanTracy watched Rize work out on the horizon ridge (a place for training), Juan-Tracy fell off a broken tree branch out of excitement and observation of Rize's tremendous fight tactics on Horizon Ridge obstacle course. "Ouch!" he cried.

Juan-Tracy was sure Rize didn't see him and he was right. Juan-Tracy wasn't seen, but heard! Juan-Tracy's behavior and instincts were equal with animals because he enjoyed how well they shared their space, worked together, and had survival skills to teach mankind how to coexist. He admired them for working together as friends, and that the rules of survival were matched by the bountiful! He learned to communicate with them by learning their ways of interacting.

He could mimic the animals, *flap*, *clap*, and *tap* to live in harmony. "Hey who's in the field there? Don't run! My fight is not with you!" Juan-Tracy was buried in leaves and branches. Rize was a warrior and could detect sounds of a humming bird that took a sip of nectar from a flower. Juan-Tracy was laying lifeless and steady but baffled mentally that he was heard nearly a quarter of a mile yelling "Ouch!" from that distance. "I know you are here, I can hear and feel your heartbeat! Choose or lose! Last chance!" Rize was not only a warrior but also playful at heart.

He wore a grin of confidence mostly and could feel something kind and graceful in the rhythm of Juan-Tracy's heart! "Without moving, you can hear the words coming out of my mouth?" said, Juan-Tracy!

"Why, yes!" and Rize held his stance like a warrior, "Can't everybody?"

A tear entered his eye. Outside of animals, Juan-Tracy had never bonded with anyone other than his parents that died long ago while on assignment to remove Romondon's father from his throne!

Warlords were directed by a mastermind wizard. His name was Romondon! Romondon's father once ruled the Land of Reason by painting the castle gold and had the villagers love for luster turn in their possessions of gold to maintain visible power that reflects from the castle onto the villagers and appreciation for the energy that shines throughout land. This teacher of rule separated people by standards of their mind and not of their heart!

King Dontavius of Kindness replaced him because the people valued the energy and spirit of their children and demanded rules that exemplify nature and kindness. Discovery of God given gifts for children and their children made the land proud.

And so, Romondon's father was cast out forever and his powerful spells of golden reflection in time, lost its luster in dust! His young son, Romondon, the offspring, promised to avenge his father's treatment and stole King Dontavius's daughter and took her to earth to remove all that was good from both worlds: Kindness!

Fear is an emotion. People fear what they don't understand. Perhaps UFOs are a good example because they are the most misunderstood and rightfully so. Become curious; ask questions like who, where, why and how the unidentified flying object arrived. Finally—the purpose! Find the purpose and beyond the image and the mystery is solve. Having confidence but use caution! Find an adult before anything! If a peer tries to intimidate you with fear tactics, be humorous like, "Menzy!"

Menzy is a great remedy to intimidation. Menzy is the character in this story and you will meet him soon! He's never afraid and if he is, one never knows because of his sense of humor and his ability to laugh at the faces of intimidators because it weakens their powers! Laugher is great medicine and by finding what's is silly in characters is their inability to penetrate your shield of kindness.

A smile of confidence, not making eye contact, shows you are not amused by their silliness of negative attention they seek, a sign to the intimidator your valuable time will not be wasted, and a warning for them to back off. Taaadaaah!

Juan-Tracy was no longer afraid but felt he made a friend. Juan-Tracy shared his story of his upbringing among the animals. He feared being unacceptable by others. He chose to live with animals because they did not judge.

Juan-Tracy explained that although he could not speak, his sight was extraordinary. He could see far better than any eagle or condor! Rize told JuanTracy that he was one of God's favorites—a hero!

His gifts were for others to learn from and how one sense could favor over others. Rize extended his hand of friendship and assisted JuanTracy up to his feet. "The mind is powerful but the heart gives it strength! I rise and speak to your heart! Juan-Tracy!" JuanTracy fought his tears! They modeled kindness! Juan-Tracy asked if he could assist in anyway and he in return promise to be loyal. Rize told Juan-Tracy he could use him as a navigator and how his skill of extraordinary sight was useful! Agreed!

The sound of the bell coming from the phone rang extra festive because it was Christmas morning! "Mom, can we come downstairs yet? Mom, Mom, Mommy, Mommy, Mom, Mom, Mommy! Can we come down yet! Mom, Mommy! Mom! Mom-may! Mom!" said Coodie. The world's longest phone call! It had to be a minute long! "Mom!"… I think you get the picture! "No he doesn't live here!

Wrong number!" *Bang!* went the phone to the hook. Coodie heard that before and maybe because it was Christmas, the sound of the phone slamming to the hook resonated into Coodie's memory. But who would be calling so often? What did they want? Worst time for the phone to ring.

"Mom, can…"

"Yes come down now!" The phone call nearly destroyed Christmas spirit! Coodie went to his mother and ignored the Christmas gifts. "Mom, is everything okay? Please do not say we are moving again."

"We are not going to move, and everything is fine."

Coodie knew again that everything was neither fine nor okay. Whenever, mom said "fine," things were not okay! Coodie offered to wash his mother's feet. Washing her feet made her feel better and when his mother refuses, it made her smile at least. "Go open your gifts, its fine." Coodie began to feel the energy extending out the ends of his fingertips! Eyes as wide as a goose getting chased by a crocodile! "My bike! My bike!" Hooray!

No, Not exactly!

Not this Christmas. Coodie did not have the Christmas he dreamed of. The phone ringing did actually happen and asking to wash feet was the day before Christmas. So let's rewind to the day before. Coodie's brother whispered to Coodie to follow him into the house and into the bedroom like he was a spy.

Friends and family members are sometimes tough to figure out. Learn the scientific method in this case: Who, what, where, why, how, and apply your senses with experiments! Family is the same blood and blood is thicker than water. The pain of disappointment hurts more from family because their job is to be family, which is supposed to spell loyalty! A rule of thumb is to trust God! Friends do come and go. A friend will remain your friend even during a disagreement.

A rule of thumb for a friend: to question their intentions always, and question if they have the same goals as you always. Your friend is there for you during good times and bad. They will encourage you and if they try to discourage you, ask yourself questions because friends don't discourage unless your safety is at risk or your decisions are negative! Taaaadaaaaahhh!

Coodie instantly connected to the idea of creeping on the tippy-toes, especially on the day before Christmas! He felt what Santa felt when delivering toys for Christmas! Then it hit Coodie: he recalled his sister told him a couple Christmases ago how there was no man in a red suit. "Why are we sneaking around?" Coodie asked his brother.

"Because it's a secret and follow me."

Coodie loved his brother but anything different from normal conversation was either a swift smack on the head or bad news. Coodie followed his brother and agreed to walk on tippy toes. Reality followed each step until Coodie began to stomp and have an attitude! "Okay tell me now!"

"Shhh a little more."

Coodie and his brother barely made it to the front door. Coodie felt bad news written all over the place! Coodie might as well head to the principal's office for something he didn't do. He didn't even care how loud he was! "Just tell me! Give me the prison sentence, is it life without parole?"

At the top of the steps that lead to the bedroom, it hit Coodie! "I didn't get a bike!" Coodie's volume could be heard across the street! Disappointment was an understatement! "No!

You got a bike! Now be quiet!"

"I DID?!"

"Yes! Shhh!"

"So why are we whispering?" I believe Coodie's brother got more fun out of this Christmas Eve than his own presents all together.

"Yes, but—"

"But what?!"

Coodie's hero powers kicked in even when he didn't want them too. Before he could open his mouth, Coodie already guessed that the bike was not a 10-speed. His brother took him to see the bike. The hallway walk was 12 feet, but it felt like the length of a football field. When the door opened, the lights were not on and for that instant, Coodie prayed his brother was joking but he wasn't.

The bike was a "black school bus." That was the name that is given by the neighborhood bears to describe the type of bicycle because they were used in movies when the bears missed the school bus. It was a black bicycle that is black, plain with straight handlebars, and a horn. They were popular before the 10-speed invention. 10-speed represented an upgrade technology to look better, ride, better with shift gears past 10! The expression "10 speed" stuck to its description! And with "monkey bars!"

That was also the name of the handlebars of the "10 speed." Coodie's eyes were priceless. His brother held his laugh as long as he could. All of two seconds to see the "black school bus!" It was a 3-speed with adjustments for 5-speed.

When Coodie's brother, Carlos, closed the door to turn the lights in his mother's room. Coodie felt his life ending with it. The night before Christmas had a wall to climb. The hallway walk of despair felt like 50 football fields to his room! Carlos said, "I showed this too you because you must pretend to be happy!" A show of kindness indeed by Coodie's older brother! His hero powers were very considerate and thoughtful!

The older brother's kindness is very important and his leadership behavior plays an important role in the order of his or her age. If the older sibling is not respected, it's because of his leadership and guidance. The older brother is supposed to model what's right by his older siblings or parents so the youngest in line will learns how to behave. If the order is broken so is the relationship! The regrets are not good because the youngest in line will never forget as adults and visiting or spending time will greatly reduce! Be firm but be kind leaders! Words to live by.

The morning of Christmas was here! Coodie woke up hoping he was having a bad dream. It hit him that the long walk of shame became real when he heard…

Knock! Knock! "Can Coodie come out?"

That was the first time Coodie's friend walked into his house— the indicator of a rough day of Christmas. Christmas was the day to celebrate the birthday of Jesus Christ. Gifts were exchanged, sharing of stories, sharing meals, spending time with family, friends as well as reflection of those who were no longer with us in Bearsville.

CHAPTER FIVE

The reflection of the "black school bus" baffled Coodie and he applied science to the questions in his mind. At his age and what he understood was, "Exchanges of gifts are a testament of good behavior. If you were naughty, your friends knew and fewer gifts were under the forest tree."

How was Coodie going to live this one down and get over it? Coodie was a good apple bear cat kid. And by the way, Coodie was an apple bear cat kid and the entire world was apple bears! Unfortunately in the future, the effects of turmoil, the level of love and kindness for mankind went into darkness and self-destruction! The offspring of people mutated into apple bear cat kids and a host of bully bears!

Rumor had it: the rulers from many countries ignored the warning signs from land animals, birds, and animals from the seas. They forgot to care about the destruction of trees and the global warming effects. Was Christmas not going to have the same traditions?

How was Coodie going to live this one down and get over it? By deductive reasoning the other purpose for not getting the gift that is wished for had to be either for bad behavior or "no money!" Coodies's friends woke up bright and shiny, but for Coodie it was not a bad dream that morning and Coodie did not race out of bed. Coodie covered himself deeper into the covers. "I don't want Christmas to come," said Coodie. Well at 10 years old, feeling noble wasn't the first thought! Carlos said, "Get out of bed before Mom finds out you don't like your bike."

"I don't like it!" said Coodie.

Coodie finally got out of bed and took the walk of despair. Got cleaned up, dressed and his friends were waiting on the street corner with the best and most colorful 10-speeds money could buy! Coodie went back inside to look at his "black bus" to compare and almost began to cry. Coodie looked over his shoulders before turning around and his mother uttered the words, "Merry Christmas, cutie!"

Coodie gathered every drop of happiness in his body and the weight of the world included to assist in his smile. Coodie forgot to get the frog sound of sadness out of his voice! "Hi, Mom! Merry-lend-money, I mean, Merry Christmas!" Coodie said.

"Are you okay, cutie?" said his mother.

"I'm fine," said Coodie. Coodie checked for acceptance of pretending to be happy by his brother's reaction. His brother gave a downward head-nod of approval! It made Christmas a lot better. Coodie promised himself to never hurt his mother's feelings and to follow directions. Coodie knew his respect for his mother was very important. Life was tough and a child's role was to obey his parents.

Always respect your parents and adults. It's never cool to embarrass your parents, family members, or friends! Kindness does not define this type of behavior! Trade places with the person you interact with to treat them the way you want to be treated. People see how you treat others and it may be funny to put others down but in the long run of the analyses, people see how you will treat them if they are smart!

A rule of thumb is threat others as if you want their child to learn from what you taught them! Taaadaaaaaaaaah!

Besides, Mother Bear was the only one that was taking care of the family of five and it was hard work to deal with behavior issues, plenty of mouths to feed, and a lot of toys to buy or get from Santa Bear.

Coodie further applied unselfish reasoning to cope with disappointment. Rather than complain or act as the victim, he used his heart and mind to accept his mother's decision on the positive side of reasoning even on Christmas.

Coodie turned around and his brother took the bike outside already! Coodie was in total shock. "You took my bike outside already …thanks!" Coodie had to remember that his mother was near him. Coodie's best friends were waiting at the corner and his mother was at the door behind him. Coodie got on the bike then got off the bike. "Is the bike working okay?"

His brother gave the all-clear sign with thumbs up! Coodie got back on the bike and rode on the sidewalk next to cars that are parked to hide the black-bus! "Come on, Coodie. We've been waiting as promised. Remember we said we will all meet…what!"

The laughs and whispers. Loud whispers and Coodie heard laughing and saw hands covering over the mouth and Coodie had no more cars to hide behind as he rode on the sidewalk rather than the streets. The black bus and Coodie made what became an embarrassing Christmas the most fearless Christmas of all time each peddle and each car he passed. There was no more care and Coodie cared less about his feelings and kept his focus on what was dear to him, his love for his mother and not wanting to hurt her feelings! Once Coodie lined up next to his friends, one of them said, "It's fine!"

Coodie said, "No it's not!"

And one by one, they all began to ride their 10-speed bike with amazing colors! The sounds of laugher grew with each peddle.

Coodie knew they could ride but one by one, the ability to ride was a difficult task. Coodie could see and hear the laughter from his friends that road like a squiggly chalk line two miles per hour and one at a time! Coodie held his head up took two trips, down and back down and back. It was luck or misfortune but the chain broke while peddling on the third trip on the black bus.

Coodie put his bike away for another day—an unselfish act for the concern of others is kindness but Coodie accepted that misfortune as fortune of dignity. "Sorry, Mom, but the bike is broken and besides, I have other presents to play with," said Coodie. Coodie went inside with a mustard smile.

Christmas day turned to Christmas night in his eyes. Coodie watched his friends ride their bikes from the foggy window and through the Christmas lights blinking around him. Even the television did not interest him, except for the stream of light that entered earth's atmosphere the other night in Bearsville.

The rest of his day included an hourly pretentious smile to ensure his mother did not feel the sadness in her heart.

The ability to overcome hurt will make you stronger. Deep breathing and saying calm. Empathy works during confusion or when you feel mistreated and not revenge! Intentions maybe at your best interest but a second time encourages you to ask questions! Arm yourself against life's endeavors! Let negative tones and comments or words bounce off your heart of armor! Letting everyone in your heart is too heavy. A penny of love at a time inside your heart's piggy bank of trust is a good pace. Deposit and withdraws are based on how well they spend their time with you! Life is how well you plan in most cases. Experience as a teacher and let people teach you lessons of what and what not to do in the future! Taaaadaaaaah!

It hit Coodie in the late evening. The night before Christmas day, he always sang "Silent Night!" Coodie always kept God in his heart. A strong believer in Jesus as the son of Mary and Joseph! Coodie began to feel inspired to sing his favorite song, "Silent Night."

He went to his room opened the window to sing. First he sang the original song of "Silent Night" followed by the remake of "Silent Night" by the Temptations! Coodie's mother came into his room to say goodnight with a smile! "I haven't heard you sing since you were five years old with the family's gospel group. Do you remember the words that set the church to start shouting, Cutie? 'Something about religion that I just don't understand but I got it!' "I do, Mom," said Coodie.

We were wearing white suits and were dressed sharp as a bear claw! Coodie loved his mother. She kissed him and said, "Goodnight." But the night wasn't over for someone else that was overheard Coodie singing Christmas carols! I could tell you who but it's time for a cup of tea! Just kidding! If you guessed that it was Rize that heard Coodie singing Christmas carols and gospel music, then you are right!

Rize is not only a warrior with a great heart with purpose to find his sister that was taken to earth by evil Romondon but also find the one "Coodie" with the same heartbeat as Rize!

Romondon's intentions were to destroy Earth? No! His intentions were to draw the goodness in the hearts of people to prove to the king on Planet Reason that he was wrong to take over his father's place as ruler long ago! The king's daughter was the light—that was all that he had left to keep Planet Reason glorious with love and kindness.

The king missed all of his children and their hearts for quality of mankind. He misses his children the most as it affected the weather: his love for his son and his daughter. His love for his daughter and her heartfelt kindness was strongest! Kindness empowered his son as his love and passion for peace guided him and kept his heart firm but calm as it beat for the safety of his best friend. Her heart was pure and powerful on all sides with love and kindness for all just like her father!

Juan-Tracey told Rize where the slap-boxing matches were held in Bearville to help narrow his search. Slap-boxing was a form of boxing but without boxing gloves. It was known to settle differences among the bears or to simply have fun.

It had been scored by the amount of hits to the face. "Love taps on the face by the apple bears is where you think I should look," said Rize.

"Yes, it a rush of excitement and bears have fun earning points for slaps to the face. It's a friendly expression of sport and honor among the bears."

"That sounds like Powton on the land of Reason," said Rize.

"Exactly," said Juan-Tracy.

"They hug, shake hands, and it builds lasting relationships among the bears," said Juan-Tracy.

Rize had no choice but to attend. The event kept his energy flowing and his strength up. "It provided clues to his search for Coodie, at the very least if he's not there," said JuanTracey.

His spirits provided nourishment for the princess if she was nearby to absorb it. "This energy lets me recuperate," said Rize.

"Agreed," said Juan-Tracey.

He refused to let any sadness enter his heart for fear of loss of energy for the princess and his planet that desperately needed his help. He became distracted by a slap-boxing match in the park. In the crowd were cheers from the slap-boxing match in the park. He could feel a surge of energy coming from them. It was the same kind of energy the he felt from the princess before her capture! It struck Rize with the answer of the obvious. Crowd excitement would lead a field of energy that would keep the balance of power to his favor! He went to investigate.

Rize knew that if he focused on Christmas carols, this was his best chance to find kindness in the heart of who they called "Coodie." Rize informed Juan-Tracy that he found Coodie and that he will let him know that he will follow Coodie for a while to discover why his heart of kindness is great and why their hearts beat at the same time.

Romondon was detecting a presence of his species on Earth. He looked into his ring of magic to investigate. The image showed a presence, but he could not determine who. Romondon already began to organize his infiltration of spells to place on the minds of apple bears! "I will start with people of authority and work my magic on the citizens last! Ha ha haaaaaa!" Romondon flew over government buildings, police stations, transportation systems, then pointed is ring at the clouds that changed the color from white to dark gray. His plan was working to perfection.

Romondon's torch of disparage already took its form of destruction and mistrust that affected the minds of bears. The changes of heart in good apple bears became swayed to evil-minded apple bears. Rather than the truth that was written in speech, it turned to blame and deceit: riots, pickets, and traffic tickets designed to increase tension and opposition. It is written: A speaker's eyes were rerouted to speak of despair and destruction.

Picketing, opposition, and mistrust became the result of misguidance and spells! Fights among the bears increased at sports events with spectators at home and abroad affected with frustration rather than sportsmanship and lack patience roamed the air and returned to fight and argue. People stopped waiting in line for their food and traffic jams increased. Their hearts were turning cold.

47

CHAPTER SIX

Their minds became sponges as they soaked up fear and anger. The princess was still locked up in a small room in the same church that Coodie attended and he didn't have a clue of his purpose yet! Christmas break was over and Coodie had school in the morning.

"Wow, look, Mom. Ali-bear got moves. He inspires me. He's amazing! The media can't see that Ali-Bear is talking to us little bears about how great he is and I see his kindness. Mr. Ali-bear is greatest slap-boxer of all time!"

"Who are you talking about, cutie?"

"Mr. Ali-bear, Mom, on television. He won last night."

Mother said, "Tell Mr. Ali-bear you have school now. The greatest slap-boxer of all time wants you to go to school and learn something!"

Coodie finished his honey and biscuits, kissed his mother on the cheek, and headed to school. Little did he know that he had Rize above him, is keeping an eye on him. Juan-Tracy informed Rize that not much time was left before Ronmondon would find his whereabouts and he reminded him to beware of his evilness. "Gotchu!" Rize reported.

Read and become inspired by learning about people that touch the lives of others, and allow their aspirations to assist you with your future goals too. Parents and friends think about your friends, or family members and what they enjoy most. They could be struggling with what they want to become in life. For example, if they enjoy cooking perhaps share what you discovered that excites them or a relative habit that is positive. Technology is a tremendous source for researching skills that match careers. It could be their gift from God. They will appreciate you for your sincerity. It also shows you care and that you have best interest at heart. Taaaaadaaaaaah!

Coodie's friend, Menzy, was hiding behind a car to sneak up on him. Rize began to counterattack Menzy as he began to spring into action. Menzy had been Coodie's friend since he moved into the neighborhood.

Menzy was a 13-year-old boy that was immune to bullying with a whacky cartoonish sense of humor.

Menzy stood up to bullies and didn't realize it until he got away.

A bully met him in the boys' bathroom in school one day and told Menzy to hand over his lunch money. Menzy said, "Okay I'm going into my pockets now and about to take out MY MONEY! (Loudly so someone could hear him.)" Menzy reached in pocket to take out his lunch money. "OKAY, I'M GOING INTO POCKET NUMBER ONE, TWO, THREE, AND BACK POCKET NUMBER FOUR!" Nothing came out.

The bully began to grow impatient and annoyed. Threats began to fly from the bully's mouth. "I'm giving you ten seconds or I will rip each hair off you and serve you up!"

Menzy looked at the bully and said, "Rip each hair off?? How you gonna do that? You can't eat a bear!"

The bully began to walk towards Menzy to do harm. Menzy said, "Oh I know where my money is, wait!" The bully stopped in his tracks.

Menzy took his shoe off. The Bully began to make a fist and the school bell rang and students entered the restroom. Once Menzy saw additional students he ran out with one shoe in his hand! Menzy made a clown face at the bully and fled. He hid a gold coin in the back of his ear! "I'll see you again!" the bully yelled.

"Okay, your mama bear said to be sure to eat your porridge and keep your promises, boo!" Menzy screamed at Coodie from behind and Menzy tooted! "Don't do that!"

Rize agreed as he took a reversal move that propelled him in a dive roll to avoid making contact against Menzy. Coodie laughed so hard he tooted too. Juan-Tracy asked, "What's a toot?"

Rize said, "Yuck! You don't want to know!" They both laughed as they realized they had the exact same breakfast! "Should we pick up Gina? She should be ready this time. She promised."

"Okay," said Menzy. Coodie and Menzy spotted Gina heading in the direction toward them but did not see them and they hid to scare Gina.

Menzy tugged on Gina's hair and said, "Boo!"

Gina turned around and socked Menzy on the mouth! "Ouch! What did you do that for?" yelled Menzy. "That's for pulling my hair and teasing me while you were riding your bike the other day! I told you I was going to get you one day. Now it's here!"

"Psych-yo-mind dat!" It was easy to see that Gina was never afraid of anyone.

Her favorite word, "All ma-life I had to fight and I don't mind doing it again!"

Menzy didn't get that Gina meant what she said. "Hi Coodie!" Gina liked Coodie since day one. Rize was quickly learning a strange ritual of greetings for these characters. JuanTracy asked what just happened. "Is the bear they call Coodie under attack?"

"No, another bear is playing, a psycho mama!"

"What does that mean?"

"Not sure. There is much to learn here about apple bear cat kid behavior." Coodie, Menzy and Gina were inseparable. The forces would have them in the same class together at school. Schools had apple bear cat kids that wanted to learn and then there are apple bear bully boys that enjoyed negative attention a bit too much and would rather spend their day antagonizing others!

Menzy and Gina were at it again with name calling to see who could handle a good insult the best. Menzy decided he had enough insults, hit Gina, and took off running. "I'm gonna get you in class!"

Menzy was determined to get Gina to like him but Gina would never allow that to happen. "If mind don't matter, the matter don't mind you, Menzy!" Gina made a fist instead of open hands and Menzy backed off from Gina. Menzy loved Gina but Gina loved Coodie and loved peace. He enjoyed finding the best in people and making it known. He appreciated the world around him. He became one with nature and found his strength from the kindness of others or will model what it looks like.

Coodie's heart was so big, he encouraged all bears to learn and work together.

"Long day, I'm bored," said Coodie.

Coodie went back to tossing rocks at cans in the park as the lady bear walked past him with a small pet or something that's furry. Suddenly she reappeared after walking past and unwrapped the furry animal that is tucked inside a cardboard box! It turned out that it was a puppy!

She offered the furry pup to Coodie and said she had no use for it. Coodie was at a loss for words. "But, but… what? Oh, it's so cool!" He stated that he would. Coodie got his very own puppy for the first time. He had to come up with a name for him because the lady left in a hurry and never told Coodie what his name. Coodie looked in his eyes and said, "Blue! I will name you Blue." Blue brought attention wherever Coodie took him.

Everyone fell in love with Blue. Coodie didn't have a leash for him because where ever Coodie went, Blue was sure to follow closely. Blue loved to play activities like fetch.

Blue was very stubborn when it came to staying put at bedtime. He never liked staying alone in the yard. He'd cry until someone came to reassure him he would be safe. Blue was a fast learner.

One day while walking on the way to the park with Blue, Coodie and his apple bear friends played keep away. Blue rarely interacted with other dogs as a pup but once he got a little older he could not avoid making friends with other dogs and bears too. He would rush to meet big dogs, short, fat, tall. or skinny dogs too. Blue loved the park and Codie took blue every day after school. Dogs seemed to have a way to bring people together. They had many qualities. They were loyal, friendly, playful, and loved to run, explore, and most of all they showed us how we should get along.

One day, watch how well they play when they are around other dogs and people to see for yourself!

"Big day today!" Gina told Coodie and Menzy about the yearly announcement in school that day.

"Our principal announces over the intercom that we are going to kick off the slap-boxing tournament that is held at the gymnasium. Three prizes, three beautiful 10 speed bicycles, three checkers and chess sets, and tickets to Honey Apple Bear Amusement Park!"

"How did you know Gina?"

"I heard them talking about it in the office when our teacher, Mr. G, sent me on an errand. The principal told his secretary and I was standing there." Gina made every attempt to share the news that Ali-bear would also be meeting with the winners, but Menzy distracted her all the way to school. Coodie thought to himself, how great it would be to win that 10 speed bicycle.

Coodie imagined himself from running with great leaps and bounds with each step and imagine himself riding the great 10-speed bicycle is even better! "How do I win? I mean how do we join up!"

"You join up by having a team of three with one girl on each team."

Coodie could hardly think in school. All he could imagine was winning the 10-speed bicycle and taking his mother to the amusement park. The janitor that carried an odor coming from his breath, snapped him out of his vision. "Excuse me, I'm just here for the trash basket." No one had seen this janitor before and neither did Coodie. Coodie, with his kind heart, raced to grab the trash basket for him. "Thank you, kind sir," said the janitor. "I have a treat for you!"

Coodie told the janitor, "No thanks. I don't mind getting the trash basket at all."

"Are you sure? It's free for your effort."

Coodie had already raced back to his seat. Rize stood in the back of the class observing the behavior of the students. He noticed a bully bear staring at Coodie and could read his racing heartbeat.

CHAPTER SEVEN

Rize was not visible to anyone. His visibility would create unwanted attention and he remembered what his king said: "they fear what they don't understand." the door shut tight.

Unusually tight as if someone was not happy! Mr.G was teaching his lesson to the class and did not see who entered the classroom. "Who came to the door?" he asked. Coodie said it was the new janitor. Mr. G carried on with his Science lesson about magnets and its attraction of negative and positive magnetic fields. Mr. G loved his job.

He believed in the quality of education and that every apple bear cat kid should value education. "Education is the honey to a good job." Mr.G gave tickets and prizes to his students every ten minutes for focusing on learning! One day, Mr. G gave twenty tickets to each student!

He told the class, "We are all working together at the same time," and if his arms were wide enough and long enough, he would gather the students up and give a big hug! Then he gave everyone a treat! The kids signed their tickets and put them in the spinner to see who won prizes!

Kids like knowing that teachers care. It makes them feel appreciated for working just like the real world. Good managers equals a happy employee.

If you guessed that the janitor was Romondon that tried to bribe Coodie, you are right! Romondon got word from his bully boys about Coodie having a big heart and attempted to hand Coodie sleeping poison mixed in his candy. *Never take candy from strangers!* Romondon threw his janitor's uniform on the headed of the current janitor's sleeping head and fled. "I will catch this Coodie one day."

His energy of kindness was preventing the speed of destruction and evil. Rize continued staring at a bully boy that was staring at Coodie and followed him as he exited the classroom.

Rize's powers prevented him from discovering his past but he could predict his future. The bully boy Darondon met with several other bully boys and inquired who Coodie was and where he was from! The bully boys had not heard of Coodie before and decided to see him again with mean intentions! This was the kind of behavior Rize had seen before in his

Land of Reason. Although Rize could not see the janitor's face, it triggered his reflection!

How was he blind from the safety of his best friend's, the princess, kidnapping in such a manner? Hiding in the mist was Romondon! He was in search of the princess. Romondon's search was over. He nabbed the princess by putting a hood over her face and ran off with her. Just then before the end of the festive games on the Land of Reason rumbles of the ground distracted him.

Cracks in the grown said Rize and Romondon was winning in the festive games but because of the roar of winds, and increasing cracks, both competitors sought refuge! People ran for their lives and Rize raced feverishly to find his friend the princess.

Rize began to realize that his friendship and appreciation for the princess had grown.

The princess screamed for her life. With her eyes blocked from a sack that covered her, "Release me at once you there with a cold heart!" Romondon continued his ride with disregard. She poked a hole in the seams of the sack she with her finger tips. "I demand that you release me at once and you will be forgiven for this dishonorable sin!" Rize searched for detail in his reflection to assist him with dealing with Coodie's plight!

The princess had enormous effects on Rize with her encouraging words of thought. Rize could be boastful with overconfidence! He recalled a time that supportive words touched his heart: "Learning from the eyes of another may open your heart to what is possible from this Land of Promise!" Rize learned a lot of what the princess told him. Once he climbed a tree with ease and threw himself on a wild horse! The horse threw him at every attempt.

The begrudging horse had personal issues with Rize and he was amused by Rize's attempt to ride him with no kindness applied. On his last attempt, the horse stood watching Rize's next strategy to ride him. Rize was rubbing his backside and began to apply a strategy of kindness! Rize walked slowly toward the side of the horse's sight for to be seen and held his hands below his waist with open palms! Rize said, "Please sir may I have a feather from the back of your tail!" The horse threw his tail hair and wacked him on the face.

Rize fell backwards to the ground. Finally, Rize realized that kindness works but kindness is needed to apply to the situation in a proper manner. Rize stood up with confidence, positive gestures, and spoke from his heart. He walked slowly towards the powerful horse with his hands to his side with open palms and said, "I would appreciate your assistance to help save the princess. It is far away; it would take me days by foot but hours with a ride from you.

Blessed be the one that is unafraid to share your gifts for love of others!" The powerful horse kneeled and gave Rise a ride.

The other horses were amazed and so were the other animals who witnessed Rise's kind words!

As he rode off Rize said, "Together we Rize!" On his way to the castle, Rize saw a man in old clothes with deep sadness on his face. It was King Dontavius! Rize was unaware that he was him and stopped to give the king water by the river and food to eat. Rize's love for mankind had changed him from the words of the princess and the behavior of animals when kindness was applied.

Rize asked the king if he knew what happened to the land. He told the king that he heard amazing stories from a beautiful amazing girl and all he could see was a land of destitution. The king was distraught and could barely speak. Each uttering word caused in a distance the ground to tremble and crack. The king said, "I'm saddened by many things!

The belief in all things has left me and my stories no longer has meaning! Each story that is shared by me is used by others in the wrong manner!"

This land that was once filled by love and kindness was successful through his queen's heart and the people that keep kindness alive. A speaker of my stories must be honorable by making his castle look like his kingdom! A boy was a child of God and is ordained to keep what is taught that is good in his heart! He relied on the guidance of goodness and kept what was kind as his outgrowth and upbringing!

Without kindness are unspeakable things! Keep that is good and listen to your heart.

"I am love!" said the King.

Rize said to the man, "You must be a King!"

Rize accepted every word and asked if he could help the king. The king told Rize to find the princess because she was what was left of him that was good! "Kindness must return here for the safety of both worlds!"

Rize rode off. He relied on faith. All things of living life are lived through the harmony of nature.

Rise's heart grew with understanding and his self-awareness and connection of what is greater filled his heart. He followed his heart. "We must be sensitive to animals. They teach us many things! To ignore animals is to ignore me! For nature is the key to define kind spirit! Nature is in all to embrace and not erase. While on his travels." *Ring*! The school bell woke Rize his dream.

Word began to spread about the slap-boxing tournament and that Coodie and his friends were going to join. Coodie and his friends were heading home from school to discuss the possibilities and it went this way: "I can't slap box," said Menzy.

"Me neither but how hard could it be?" said Coodie.

"You both are silly! Just like this!" *Pow!* Gina slapped Coodie and Menzy on the face!

"Ouch! That hurt."

"Well if it hurts then maybe you shouldn't join!"

CHAPTER EIGHT

"All my life, I had to run," said Menzy, "and I've gotten pretty good at dat! We should learn, practice, and hard work on the technique that the greatest Ali-bear teaches on television! Why don't we pray about it and talk about it. Right now?" said Menzy.

Slap! "No silly, when you get home!"

"Why not right now?" The three apple bear cat kids stopped in their tracks, held hands right there and Coodie started the prayer: "Dear Lord, protect us from evil and if we could learn how to slap box may we only learn to defend ourselves and never hurt anyone that don't have it coming to 'em. Amen!"

Coodie often challenged his gifts of understanding the hearts of his friends and whom he met. His influences came from superheroes and sports figures. He read books and comic book and opened his mind to what was impossible to the possible.

In fourth grade, Coodie realized that if he got his schoolwork done early, he could have free time. His teacher had board games and magnets in the back of the class to play with. It was all he needed to know as a motivation. There was never enough classwork that could keep him from earning free time.

Soon as he was done he raced to play with magnets and marbles. The magnets made what was impossible possible to his imagination. Anything that was magnetic was intriguing and how things that possess the opposite needed additional discoveries! Coodie loved his teacher for having something that motivated him to complete work.

Just then, in the background stood Darondon, he was following the three bears! If you guessed that Darondon was the same boy from the party of several year ago, you would be right! Derondon's aunt and uncle were raising him because his parents were hurt badly in a car accident the day they left home for the party. Darondon blamed Coodie. His parents attended a party that same night and had too much to drink that day.

When Darondon was picked up he was thrown from car and was badly bruised. Derondon's parents had been attending therapy for several years now and were expected to see him soon. Derondon was unaware that his aunt and uncle were a bad influence on him. Darondon wants revenge!

Coodie's mother chose to walk Coodie to school on his first day. His mother was bothered by multiple phone calls to the family's home. Coodie was asking his mother, "Why are you walking me to school and why are we going this direction? Mom, my school is this direction."

Coodie's mother said that she wanted him to go to a different school. Coodie always respected his mother and never wanted to disappoint her. He did beg his mother if he could go where he promised his friends that he would see them again. His mother said she believed the new school will be a better fit. Coodie was very sad and he accepted her decision and hoped to change her mind. Coodie was close to his mother.

While on the way, Coodie had another daydream. He reflected to the day he washed his mother's feet. He took out a bucket of water and a cloth and asked his mother to put her feet in the bucket right out in the public. Coodie's mother was happy. She cried easily and it was plain to see that they were tears of joy. Coodie hoped that his mother would also reflect and not worry.

"Mom, Mom, Mom, Mommy, Mom. Mommy, Mom, Mom, Mom-may!" Coodie's mother was on the phone. This time she was not getting off. This frightened Coodie because his mother either laughed loudly because she is talking to her friends, relatives, or to pay a bill, but never this serious and this quiet! "Mom, Mom, Mom, Mom, Mom-may!"

Nothing worked. Coodie's mom liked when he would come to her when she was on the phone too long and used him as an excuse to get off. "Coodie, what is your last name?" Coodie's eyes got wide! "Hun? Yes spell your last name?" For the first time, Coodie's hero powers went on mute! "Ah ah ah…" Coodie completely misspelled his name.

He was always ignored when his mother was on the phone and the shock was too great! His mother smiled and hung up the phone. Porridge never tasted so good that night at dinner time. Coodie had fish and porridge for dinner. It hit Coodie to tell the news of the slap-boxing tournament and right before he could speak, a chunk of fish with the bone got trapped right into Coodie's wind pipe. His throat! Little as he was at the table, he could barely look over, he immediately thought how life was about to start and now it was over!

No hero powers were going to help this time because Coodie couldn't speak. No one would see him because he was too small. No one would care because he was unimportant. Coodie began to lean over thinking he needed room to fall but with his feet dangling off the floor and choking to death, he struggled to remove himself from the table. Right there and then his oldest brother walked by him and slapped Coodie on the back.

And the chunk of fish with the bone in it came flying out! Coodie's brother's hero powers kicked in to save his little brother's life. After Coodie got his voice back, he told his brother thank you. "I was choking and you saved my life right in time."

It pays to be kind as it spreads in ways that we ever know! Pay it forward!

Was there a real slap boxing event? Did Rize inspire Coodie's oldest brother Rashad with a surge of energy from his hands to slap Coodie perfectly on the back or was it the oldest brother's obligation to protect his youngest brother? Rize observed Coodie and his mission became clearer as his heartbeat remained steady like him. Rize knew his mission and he took rest to his mind.

Rize's strength increased by connecting with the gifts of others. He realized that by listening with an open mind to the greatness of others, goodness was discovered in their heart! It came through the positive reflection of their spirit and goodwill that tugs the heart! Time was the instructor and reflective listening through the heart as it inspires the goodwill and actions of man and woman!

Saturday morning was always fantastic! Coodie loved to watch his morning heroes combat the bad guys! All of the superpowers posed and thrilling episodes from the previous Saturday kept Coodie glued to the television set! Coodie enjoyed his time on Saturday mornings. The reflective lights that bounced off the television shows that were filled with conflict and solutions with hero action-packed scenes to defend the universe and beyond excited Coodie to no end.

When Coodie watched other shows he could easily dial in the parts of shows that did things that further solve problems. Other shows that attracted his attention included the best in people and he discovered what superpowers they possessed. A great performer encourages the people to embrace and it is indicated the singer's ability to touch the hearts with love and affection.

The astronauts that made people feel proud also made people want to fly. The comedians that told jokes made them forget about worrying or fighting. The radio stations played music with words of taking a look at life and being proud made people feel they were not alone. Coodie's confidence grew when he read comic books because much of life's problems had solutions and made the heroes influence the world. Coodie went to school sharing what he often imagined what a school of successful learners look like.

A bowl of porridge and a new sheet of aluminum foil to ensure a good picture setting for a clearer image! Commercial breaks gave Coodie time to replenish and refresh himself. Coodie learned from the best of good versus evil doers and developed a good sense of morals and fortitude when decisions were made to choose to fight or wait another day minute or hour. Time was the best decision maker. Heroes with patience, style, great skills, speed, personality, smarts, self-control, analysis skills, and of course, kindness, were the best!

Every character of a hero or villain took advantage of one ingredient that decided who would win and who will lose and that is time! It was time to fight, run, react, hit, move, get help, fly away, go faster, slower, etc. Getting angry at a situation distorted reasoning like logic, understanding, and clearer thinking. Staying calm allowed blood to flow to the right areas of the body, which results in balance achieved.

Try this exercise the next time you become emotional to a negative extreme like anger, or hurt like sadness or disappointment: squeeze your abdomen muscles as if to reach your diaphragm as hard as you could for several seconds then release. This allows you to control negative or unwanted feelings in an instant! Deep breathing, of course, helps keep you calm.

Just like the great hero shows on television, it was time for Coodie bear to play with his friends! *An idled mind is the devil's workshop!* Saturdays were the best days for free time. Coodie ran to his best friend's home to build.

Coodie borrowed his older brother's hammer and let his creativity do the rest. Menzy found and old set of roller skates, and Gina found boards with nails stuck inside. Coodie found a wooden create at the back of an old warehouse. "Pass the hammer Coodie so I can take the nails out," said Menzy.

"I found more boards with nails and some without nails," said Gina.

Coodie began putting the pieces together after unscrewing the old roller skates with a piece of metal he found in the open sand lot. Coodie and Menzy began hammering nails back into the old piece of wood with the wheels and backing. "Dang!" said Menzy.

Coodie asked what happened. Menzy missed the nail on the head and banged his finger. Gina laughed so hard she fell back and landed inside the dumpster. Coodie went to help.

Gina stepped on a nail! Being carful became a difficult task but was better than sitting on the steps doing nothing. Finally the skateboard was complete. Coodie, Menzy, and Gina made a skateboard out of old pieces of wood and roller-skates. The neighbors were tickled by the minute because the skateboard began to weaken every exchange of turns riding up and down the street and because the old wood could not hold the nails very long. Gina took one last ride up the street and splat went the skateboard into pieces!

Menzy asked Coodie if applying the wooden crate would allow the skateboard to be converted into a scooter. Gina, Menzy, and Coodie had time and so they went to rebuild the skateboard to convert it into a scooter. The only difference was the crate. The three raced around the corner of the street and over to the old warehouse. Only this time, Derondon was there, watching everything from a distance where he could not be seen. Derondon raced to inform the bully boys that three bears were on their turf and wanted trouble. In those days, if you went two blocks away for your neighborhood, you better have good reason to be there or trouble would surely follow!

While the three bears were nearly completed with their project, a tap on Menzy's shoulder from one of the bully boys created what you may not expect. Especially if it was Menzy who gets tapped! "Quit it, Gina. We are working here!"

"Menzy, I'm next to you silly!" Both of the workers were looking downward.

Tap tap! "Coodie stop playing! I don't want to bust my finger again!"

Coodie was in the dumpster, looking for nails. "I'm over... Look out!" said Coodie! It was an old friend that told Menzy he would see him again and he was standing next to

Menzy only this time it wasn't Menzy that was the target; it was Coodie.

Darondon asked, "Where are you from?"

Coodie was just brushing the wood chips off his clothes and casually responding, "We live around the corner!" Derondon yelled, "No you don't; you live across the tracks, you are a gang member!" Coodie was baffled by Derondon's response and struggled to recall Derondon's voice because it was familiar to him but because they had a cloth tied around their faces, it was distorting Coodie's memory. "We live around the corner if you don't believe us feel free to follow us."

"Yeah Coodie is not lying! I mean we all are friends here and we don't want trouble do we, friends?" said Menzy as he attempted to get a hug. The bully bears walk closer to Coodie and Derondon told Coodie he knows he is a church boy, made a sign of a cross and slapped Coodie on the face!

oodie was shocked by the slap. Coodie responded by asking if he and his friends could go. The bully bears laughed and told them to never come back! Gina and Menzy attempted to console Coodie. Coodie was silent nearly the entire walk home. Coodie thought to himself the importance of turning the other cheek in the face of enemies.

Rize watched the entire event. Juan-Tracy asked Rize to intervene but Rize could see Coodie's heart and what made him so noble. Coodie thought of the safety of his friends and not himself. Juan-Tracy told Rize that he was Coodie's guardian angel! He went home straight to his room and said nothing to his family members. The one thing left on his mind was if he should allow himself to get hit on the other cheek! It was Sunday morning and time for church.

Coodie had forgotten the slap on the face and simply hoped he would never see those bully boys again. His faith was put to the test and Coodie looked at the test as if he passed. Little did he know that fate would not have his back!

Church has just started and Coodie and his family members were glad to see each other as the preacher was just about to start. Coodie felt a peace. His pastor often shared how important sacrifice is and love for one another is the life of a Christian.

Coodie smiled gallantly because the pastor's words felt close to the home of his heart. "A time to fast which is to not eat a meal sometime between now and next Sunday saints and friends!" Coodie heard the pastor share the word of not eating before by fasting! Coodie felt guilty the last time it was suggested but felt determined to follow through sometime between now and next Sunday. "It brings you closer to God and a sacrifice is good."

When Coodie left church, he and his family rode home while Coodie was silent. The family had so much to talk about from their day and besides, Coodie had the time to think. "I will sacrifice my meal this week for lunch!"

It was time for school and Coodie ate his breakfast porridge and headed to school. Menzy and Gina had already left for school. Coodie forgot about the slap incident and put the slap into a category of a learning experience to not go into the area again. The conversation continued to harp about the slapboxing tournament and that it is starting soon. Coodie, Gina, and Menzy forgot about all about it.

Coodie! Menzy's way of scaring a person without saying, "Boo!" had no effect on him. The class was fun as usual. Mr. G shared his favorite heroes growing up and could tie his lesson around any discussion. "We all have a gift from God and begin to find out your gift and let it guide you to a good job." In the corner of the class was Derondon.

He participated well that day and gave many great answers. Derondon was told by his aunt over the weekend that they were planning to move again to a new street. If you guessed it, fate did take its course.

Derondon moved just four log houses from Coodie. *Knock knock,* "It's just me. I'm here for the trash can." Coodie raced to grab the trash can, and Romondon gave Coodie the candy that was loaded with a sleeping potion mixed in it. Coodie took the candy! He wasn't thinking about what he had done! Romondon left and let out a laugh that filled the hallways with fear.

Nearly all of the classroom doors opened to see who could cause a scary sound at that level. Coodie did not eat the candy. He remembered that this is the day he would fast and skip his lunch! Rize was unaware that the janitor was Romondon because they had never met and that he was in disguise. *Ding*!

Lunch time! That instance Coodie got excited to eat and it hit him the he wasn't going to eat. However, his stomach was not fully informed. Here's how and why:

Coodie stood up and took three steps to exit Mr. G's class and a lion's roar scratched and clawed on the insides of Coodie's stomach. Coodie almost leaned over to fall and caught himself. "Are you okay?" asked Gina.

"Yeah, I'm fine," said Coodie.

Coodie remembered to fast but because he was fasting for the first time and he thought telling anybody was the wrong thing to do since it was between him and God. Each step became more excruciating than the next.

Coodie could not understand why it was happening now and other days he was fine. Not thinking that over the weekend a diet would be different from Sunday to Monday and when you change how busy from one day to another, the metabolizing system changes. Coodie managed to ignore his hunger pains and made it to the lunch room. A natural reaction for him was holding the door for his peers and greeting them as they came in and get in line himself. And he did just that.

Once his food came it hit him that he was supposed to not eat. Then the lion in his stomach growled like it was trying to literally jump out of his stomach. Cramps kicked in. Lions and cramps and tooting at the same time! Coodie took his plate, feeling more determined than before. "Ain't nothing but the devil trying to get at me!"

The second he threw his plate in the trash his stomach felt like the lion used his nail and scratched a line through his stomach.

Coodie grabbed himself with both arms wrapped around his stomach again and each step was pulling him to the ground! His classmates noticed and so did other students that were around noticed showed concern and began asking if he was feeling okay all the way to his seat. Coodie made it to his seat in the cafeteria. He began to sob as warm tears jetted out of the corners of his tear ducts! What a mess! His peers became alarmed and could not stop asking if Coodie was okay. Each time Coodie said, "I'm okay!

I'm fine!"

Gina came over and asked, "What's wrong?!"

Coodie gathered himself through the tears, "I'm fasting!" Gina asked what fasting was.

"I can't eat!"

"Why not?"

"Because I'm fasting!"

The cafeteria lady watched the entire event and raced over with another meal and went to place it in front of Coodie. With one hand, Coodie held on to his stomach and with the other hand he used it to signal a stop sign.

The cafeteria and assistant teacher were at a loss but followed through on Coodie's request. "Now if I could just sit up!" The lunch table in front of him and his shirt top was filled with tears! Gina asked Coodie to please eat and she began to cry out of concern for Coodie. At his lunch table through watery eyes of his own and feeling embarrassed and like a failure Coodie attempted to control the pain he was feeling inside.

Coodie raised his head to respond to his classmate's enormous concern and safety! They refused to eat out of concern too. Many of them left their seats and with great sympathy, the news roamed within the lunch room and the girl cubbies cried with Coodie bear. "Eat Coodie! It's Okay! Just eat!" Gina suggested that Coodie eat today and fast tomorrow. Coodie accepted the idea and it hit him that he told the cafeteria lady, "No thank you."

One of the other cubbies offered their cookie and before Coodie could count there were ten or twelve cookies and several milks! Coodie did eat and felt guilty for breaking his promise with God. He felt guilty and ashamed. Low and behold, through Coodie's foggy tears lies a corner of disappointment from one peer that sat and grew green with envy! Derondon was furious!

Rather than showing lack of empathy or sympathy to wrestle with emotionally at least become a referee to increase safety in time of crises superheroes!

School was coming to an end for the day and the speaker system beeped to make another announcement about the slapboxing tournament that would begin in a few days and to sign up soon. Coodie, Menzy, and Gina ran to the office after school to sign up for the tournament. "Ya'll sure ya'll want to sign up?" said Gina. "Ya'll can't fight! It's time we stand up for ourselves and this a great opportunity. It says here we can have a forth boxer but who will join?"

"You were ballin-ya eyes out at lunch, how you fight between tears!"

"Cry baby cry baby!" Coodie heard it all. "The janitor used a mop to collect all your tears!" It's what friends did. Coodie was well aware of "bussing," which meant to insult or name call. Take your pick. "My stomach never hurt that much before," said Coodie.

"Just fast another time," said Gina.

"I'll wait to ask my pastor when I go back to church on Sunday." While walking home Gina, Menzy, and Coodie spotted several bully boys standing on the corner near the school. They decided to take another route. "Whew just missed them."

"Ya'll need to toughin' up! Just make a fist," said Gina.

"That works for you because you have those boxing mitts for hands, Gina!"

"The better to clobber you with Menzy!"

Menzy picked up a caterpillar that was crawling on a leaf and chased Gina down the street.

"I thought you were tough!" "Why you scared of a caterpillar?" said Menzy.

"Because you ate dirt when you was a baby! Now I'm gonna get you!" Coodie laughed and went inside his home. Rize watched the entire day to learn about the behaviors that were displayed between friends and enemies. Juan-Tracy asked Rize, "Tell me what's on your mind."

"I speak from the heart, it is only the words in my mind that help me to speak! They are no different, just learning as they go! It is time that I prompt them along. The racing clouds are already beginning to create a path of destruction all over the place!"

It was already Saturday with three days to go before the tournament. Coodie skipped his Saturday morning ritual and so did his cubby buddies. Coodie came out first to pick up his friends. "Glad that's over," said a grownup as she spoke to the quiet kid from Coodie's class. If you believe its Derondon then you are right again! He lived just four houses away and it was a great opportunity to have a new teammate.

Menzy and Gina came to meet with Coodie. "Guess what? We have new neighbors and one of them is from our class."

"Well what's his name?" asked Gina.

"He's the quiet bear for the back corner of the class. He sits alone at lunchtime and he doesn't talk to any cubbies. It's a great chance to get to know him, welcome him and make a new friend," said Coodie.

"Okay, but I'm not knocking on the door." "Me neither," said Menzy.

"Okay I will," said Coodie. Coodie felt comfortable with knocking on the door until his friends became skittish. Coodie walked close to the door and before he was eight feet away, he heard lots of bears dancing and socializing and music playing. He turned around to look at Menzy and Gina. They stood in a distance with their arms folded.

"Go ahead scare-dy-apple cat!" said Menzy. Coodie could not shake the fact that his friends continued to clear themselves far away.

What did they know that Coodie didn't know? Coodie went to knock on the door. *Knock, knock*! The music stopped and feet… lots of feet went scattering as if they were going to hide. Coodie became alarmed and his hero powers kicked in. He was sure someone heard him then he heard whispering that somebody was at the door.

Coodie continued to make eye contact with his friends. They have been known to knock on doors and running for it. His head was turned toward them and just when he stretched his arm to knock he realized his hand reach well past the distance to make contact with the door. "Hello! Uh," said Coodie "We… we were wondering… my friends, I mean, we wanted to know if your son could come out and play."

"We have no son here!" And she shut the door.

Then Coodie stood silently and thought about the lady bear's answer because he was sure that he saw Derondon. Soon after the thought and while Coodie walked away, out came Derondon. Coodie turned around in his direction to introduce himself and to welcome him.

Coodie turned his head for only a few seconds and Menzy and Gina were two car distances away standing as if they had seen a ghost! Coodie set up a friendly gathering while his friends reacted with apprehension and fear!

While wearing a stone face and as if they have seen a monster, Coodie went ahead to introduce Derondon. Just before Coodie went through with introductions Derondon, "You got a problem and need to fix 'em?" Coodie was shocked by Derondon's threat but he did have a point because Menzy and Gina had the look of fear mixed with more fear by the second.

"No, they are my friends and we are hoping you will join the, "three Musketbears" and become the fourth," Coodie said. Coodie had never seen Gina afraid. Did Coodie miss a message in school or in the creepy introduction? Either way, Coodie's hero powers came in a way he didn't know.

CHAPTER TEN

I will come over and knock your head off Derondon said to his friends. Coodie's friends froze in their tracks, speechless, and Coodie's powers told him there is no time to cool down the situation any longer and it was only one thing to do. Was it the two common reactions of flight or fight?

You are right! Coodie had to do something. "Look at me," Coodie said, "We came to be friends not to cause trouble. Any further, fight me instead."

Coodie needed some way to divert Derondon's attention and it worked! Except for one thing: Derondon was now staring at Coodie with blood in his eyes! Was this what Derondon wanted all these years? After all, Derondon's life was altered on a number of incidents. Derondon first met Coodie at six months when Coodie could talk.

He stood behind him at the birthday party.

He watched Coodie get attention in the classroom and in the cafeteria. He stood behind Coodie at the Pin The Tail On The Donkey contest. Derondon attended the same church as Coodie. He even participated on his little league baseball team.

Coodie's entire life was shadowed by Derondon. Derondon was very good at sports. His hand-eye coordination was superb. He could outrun most kids in school. His spelling and handwriting was exceptional. He had a great sense of humor and girls found him to be funny. When Coodie moved to another neighborhood, Derondon's family also moved too.

Derondon was at his end as he joined the bully boys to gang up on Coodie. He could not have his life paced by Coodie any longer! His frustration and anger had been building for some time now! And Coodie told him to fight him! "Gotchya'll, don't I!" Coodie could not see it coming; perhaps it was that his heart of encouragement, kindness, and belief in mankind with positivity would not allow him to see the positivity that others represented!

For instance, while Coodie stood in line with pin the tail on the donkey contest he offered what he knew about how to win which he did but did not hear Derondon's point of view. Derondon suggested, "Winning the tail on the Donkey can happen by counting steps!"

Coodie offered Derondon the opportunity to go ahead of him and he refused. But situations like that can result in sour apples no matter how you slice 'em! There was only one thing left to do for Coodie!

Derondon had blood coming out of his eyes! His intentions were nothing short of applying his built-up pain and disappointment with an outburst of destruction! Derondon's chest expanded three times his size and his shoulder muscles grew like, "The Incredible Hulk!" His fist began to tighten as if he was gripping the chin-up bar at the playground!

Coodie immediately thought about all the heroes with speed and his favorite boxer that possessed amazing footwork and before Derondon could load up with a punch straight at Coodies face, Coodie threw a lightning right hook to Derondon's left jaw that he never saw and then a left hook! Derondon said, "Who hit me?!" Gina and Menzy immediately pointed and said at the same time.

"It was Coodie!" Gina and Menzy broke out in a laugh and as soon as the laugh started it ended because Derondon did not find the punches funny. How did Coodie respond?

If you said with kindness and are wondering how can kindness follow two blows to the face, great question. During the shock of it all and speechless behavior, time became the answer and should always, always be used as much as possible! Time is your friend. Time is not promised but if you have it, use it! Please! Coodie looked at his friend and gave him a hug! He told him he was sorry and said what his true intentions from the beginning. "Let us be friends!"

That day, Derondon accepted Coodie's hand of friendship! Character is the content of every man, woman, apple bear cat kid and bully boy! Discover the gifts in everyone and be a friend! It looks like Brotherly Love.

Derondon accepted the hug and Coodie had never been more proud! He told Gina and Menzy, "We have a fourth musketeer!" Rize took off his glasses for the first time and JuanTracey was unable to see what was happening. "What's going on? I can't see it. What's happening?"

Rize said, "Coodie wants everyone to rise and discover their gift without judgment. It is in the way we see character!"

Juan-Tracy said, "How is it that Coodie can see it when many people do not?"

Rize said, "People do and so do animals. It is the energy in our behavior. It is in the heart before the mind in that order to see. Problems are seen by many; solutions are found by few; answers are agreed by all; and truth is the last to accept!"

"Maybe that is why I was meant to not see it but needed to hear it!" Juan-Tracy said, "To understand we have eyes to see, voices to speak, ears to listen, movement for memory and they all assist us with the truth and fail to use them all. That is why you removed your glasses!" Very good. Juan-Tracy's purpose was discovered!

Coodie went on to explain to Derondon how important he was and now that he was a neighbor, time spent together being four Musketbears was greater. Derondon said, "You are pretty fast with your hands!" Coodie apologized again and asked if he was okay. Derondon replied with positive energy by smiling and participating in a game of tag!

In the background standing on the rooftop stood Romondon! Romondon also watched the engagement. He knew that if he could distract and disrupt the friendship it would create confusion and buy more time to engulf the positive energy from all the apple bear cat kid and bully boys! Romondon's plan was simply altered.

"Ah haaa!" said Romondon! He could see the negativity and lurking minds in Derondon's aunt and uncle! Their greed prevented them to see changes in Derondon and knew Derondon had avenges against Coodie.

All the while, they encouraged Derondon to forgive Coodie as it nourished Derondon's hate and now they were forced to discourage the friendship of Coodie and Derondon to keep their fortune promised by his parents' insurance money. They had to make Derondon believe that Coodie was evil to collect money and travel around the world without Derondon!

Derondon's parents suffered a terrible car accident the night of the party while on the way home. Derondon was thrown out of the car and had no memory of the incident. He was told that he was picked up by his aunt and uncle prior to the crash. Derondon's aunt and uncle were only interested in the life insurance policy with their names as the beneficiaries! If you guessed that it was Derondon's aunt and uncle calling Coodie's mother to inspire Derondon, you are right!

Derondon's aunt and uncle needed a leader for Derondon and Coodie was a good fit. They witnessed Coodie's ability to win Pin The Tail On The Donkey, Guess Where The Cup Is, and they attended Little League baseball with Derondon's parents! They called Coodie's parents to investigate his every move, pretending to be the government!

"Come on, hit me," said Coodie toward Menzy. While in back of the warehouse, two blocks around the corner from where they lived, the four Musketbears agreed that the empty lot would be an excellent place to learn to how to slap-box!

"It is time I reveal myself before they slap themselves silly," said Rize. Rize changed his clothes into regular clothes. He looked like one of the originals from centuries ago. Some of the originals lived through death, mutation, and destruction of man. Only a few were still on earth! If you noticed a change in the spelling of his name, "Rize," it is not a mistake. You too have a gift and it will be discovered if not already and after your glasses are removed let what you learn guide you, like Rise!

The four Musketbears had much work to do. Imagine a cloud of smoke and only to discover after it clears are apple bear cat kids swinging at nothing but air.

"Do something; go ahead, do something," said Gina as she held her club hand on the top of Menzy. Menzy continued to snort every five seconds. *Snort, snort, snort* while swinging with his eyes closed. Derondon laughed himself silly.

It was nice to see Derondon smile and laugh. He laughed like it had been a while and it amused him even more. "Why don't we try opening our eyes?" said Derondon.

When Menzy opened his eyes, Gina let him go and Menzy swung himself into a circle and slapped a can full of rainwater onto Coodie and the can hit Rise on the shoulder. Rise had plenty of time to react but figured that warming up to meet his new potential apprentices should happen gradually!

"Too late now! Oops sorry about dat," said Derondon! Derondon apologizing and laughing was like looking at therapy right before the eyes.

"Not a problem, caterpillar neck!" Caterpillar neck? The Musketbears broke into a roar of lighter! "Caterpillar neck? Where did you get that from?" said Menzy. And the crew laughed some more.

Menzy laughed well after everyone stopped and ended with another snort. "Was that not pleasing to laugh at?" said Rise.

"Why do you talk like dat? All proper!" said Menzy, who took leadership by initiating positive social responsibility of inviting a new potential friend in the neighborhood.

If you meet someone new and they are the same age as you, put yourself in their shoes and be polite. Making friends is difficult for some and harder for others.

"Don't crack on him with jokes" said Gina.

"Can't you see he is from another planet?" said Derondon.

Rise immediately checked his face and clothes and two seconds later, the Musketbears warmed up the new kid and asked if he had boxing skills. "Well no, but I can pick the feather off a bird… ha ha ha ha." And the Musketbears stopped and stared as if Rise was serious.

Rise stopped laughing an asked if he said something wrong. "No, we never heard that before, that's all. Where do you live?"

"I'm from down the way," said Rise, "I'm here visiting for a little while and decided to go for a walk. Boxing is fun," said Rise.

"Can you show us how to box?" asked Coodie. "We could use some help."

"Well I could show you how to slap yo mama!"

The Musketbears increasingly enjoyed the presence of Rise. Seemed like Gina made a new friend. "Yeah teach us what you know," said Gina. "Boxing is like a dance, so dance!"

"How we gonna dance without music?"

"Listen to the rhythm of your partner." "How do you mean?" asked Coodie.

"This is boxing, correct?"

"No," said the Musketbears, "In 'slap boxing,' everything is the same except hands are open."

"Well then, dance with open hands."

Derondon got angry, having a short fuse. "I'm not dancing. I'm a shifter, I change gears whenever and to whoever!"

"Classic," said Rise. "Hit me." Rise began to dance as if he was in ballet class. The others stood back to see if Derondon could slap their new friend Rise. Derondon did all he could and didn't lay fingertip on Rise. "When you move, I contract and when you contract, I expand."

"That's crack! You see dat?" says Menzy.

"Yes, I'm cracking!" said Rise. The rest of the Musketbears were ballet dancing without music. Rise inspired.

"Show us more show us more, Rise."

"Well let's catch flies!"

"What do you mean, catch flies?"

"Reading the behavior of a fly teaches speed and anticipation. One who catches a fly and releases him can have respect for bigger things." "Sounds wild, but okay," said Gina.

Now the group was catching flies. The old lady with her hair to the side was enjoying the entertainment, "There's one! Shoo fly and she slapped herself silly and her wig fell off and onto the ground. She quickly shut the window out of embarrassment. "Come on bears, you must catch one before you leave today."

Derondon caught one. Everyone ran over as if he found a gold coin. When Derondon opened his hand, nothing came out. Needless to say the bears were having fun slap boxing without slap boxing. After an hour of ballet dancing and making flies shoo instead of catching them, Rise asked the cubbies to trust him and close their eyes. Of course, Derondon had back talked. "I don't see the point to this when we need to learn slapboxing. We don't need to take a nap!"

CHAPTER ELEVEN

"Be quiet and close your eyes, I want to hear this. Okay, Derondon, observe!"

Rise closed his eyes and said, "Tune out the other sounds around you—buses, cars, birds, trees, bears, and everything else except for what matters: the flight of a fly."

Out of curiosity, a fly with round eyes came by. The four Musketbears stared intensely. You know who had to say something. "Your clothes got rust stains drying from the cup I hit you with," said Menzy!

"Be quiet," said everyone! Rise went back to his quiet place. The fly returned to his place of rest and began messaging his head. A few seconds later, his curiosity for Rise increased and the decision to see him became insatiable and flew toward Rise to get a better look at his rust stains.

He flew and several other flies followed. Rise heard the flight of the flies. The Musketbears also noticed flies that began to come from several directions! In an instant, Rise held his hand in a stop motion to prevent a fly from landing on any part of his body. The flies were bouncing off his hand as he blocked and slapped flies away like a tennis racket to a tennis ball. At last, he reached out to the first fly that initiated the attack, and caught it and brought the fly to his ear then spoke to it.

"The image is nothing more than an illusion that hides behind his true motives! Destroy the image and you will break the enemy." Romondon had sent spies to watch Rise and cast a spell on those flies.

"Wow," said the Musketbears.

That was very cool and fast at the same time. "How did you do that?" asked Menzy. "All my life I had to run!"

Rise asked the Musketbears to close their eyes. "Imagine a play and you are in the play. Imagine the fish in the stream that flows with a reflection that interferes with what you see. Look beyond the refection and you will catch the fish!" The cubbies opened their eyes and danced as if they were in a play. The flies never had a chance. One by one, they flew into the space the cubbies danced.

The more flies that came the more they fell to the hands of apple bear cat kids! Coodie walked over to Rise and asked what he said to the fly in his hand. "I told the fly, I know what you are up to," said Rise.

"Wow! I appreciate you but when do we learn how to slap box?" asked Coodie. Rise told Coodie to dance! Coodie stared the funky chicken dance. "No! Not like dat! You are in a play, so dance!"

"But how?"

"Exactly! There is no 'I'; it is we or them." So the play began and how they shaped up before to begin the play! "Now dance!" said Rise.

Coodie got into a neutral stance and did not move until Rise moved. Rise began to move and Rise threw playful slaps in Coodie's direction. The others watched.

The old lady opened window again after getting her wig from the ground. "Go Coodie, go Coodie!" she yelled and her wig slumped over her face to prevent her from seeing. She slipped her wig and it fell inside her house and the window slammed her fingers while the other Musketbears laughed! Coodie reflected on the category of his heroes.

In the process, Rise slapped Coodie on the face. "Keep your focus! What is the image?" said Rise. "I get it, can we dance again?" asked Coodie. The dance began again. Coodie began a part of the funky chicken. "Just kidding," said Coodie.

"Humor is good as it keeps good spirits and sound judgment," said Rise.

He danced as if he was in a play but this time Coodie was ready. "Slap, don't be ready. Be ready and yet be serious!"

"Yes," said Coodie, I will remember and I will practice.

"I caught a fly," said Derondon. The Musketbears came over and when Derondon opened his hands, a fly flew!

Everyone praised Derondon for his success. Derondon looked beyond the image! The Musketbears ask Rise if he would be their trainer.

They were pleased with the lessons and it was evident that Rise made quite an impression. "Yes train them they need good guidance!" said the old lady across the street as a bird flew by to snatch her wig.

The Musketbears began to give each other a nod of approval and waited for Rise to nod. I'm here for a little while before I return home from my visit. Next time we will learn how to take a feather from a bird! "Were you serious?" asked Gina.

"Why yes, pretty apprentice," said Rise.

The Musketbears thanked Rise and said, "See you tomorrow. Thank you!" Rise remained there for a while and reflected on his sister that he missed dearly. Birds, butterflies, bees, and bouquets of flowers transferred his thoughts. He could see her clearly and the most precious space in his heart. He loved his sister more than himself!

Rise's best friend, the princess, was his best critic and had her way to be his best instructor for life. "Come here take a break karate kid," his sister, Kahlia said.

"Look, see I told you there are pieces of gold in these rocks! Looking deeper into things allows you to discover more than what is on the surface. That's just a rock," said Rise.

"Don't be silly. Well come see for yourself… now look below the surface."

"Wow! How did you know?" asked Rise. "We are going to be rich!"

"But how?" his sister asked. "This is one piece."

"Well there are more where they come from, right?"

"Yes over there inside that mountain, perhaps! Now look above the mountain and what do you see? I see houses, a community where we live, love and have lived for many centuries."

"Do you want to be responsible for taking away our history and culture and way we live for gold?"

"No!" And Rise chucked the rock into the river! His sister had amazing ways to see things. A bird flew by with huge feathers! Rise tumbled with speed and extraordinary skills on top of a rock then onto a tree and over a branch to retrieve a feather from the great big bird. "Ouch!" said the bird.

"What jive turkey did a thang like dat!" Rise got distracted by two bears walking down the street and began to grin in a good way! "He's back from his reflection. Whohoo, yahoo, hoo effect of delight and skill, weee, ya gotta have fun!"

"Rise, have you learned nothing?" said Princess Kahlia. At whose expense should you sacrifice your fun for? Nature is our teacher. You rudely stole from your instructor."

And as his sister spoke, the same type of bird stood with his wings on his side in disgust. It was his mother!

The bird tapped its foot on to the ground and shamed Rise for his actions! "Please may I have a feather from your tail?" Rise stood there, regretting all the energy he spent to impress his sister for the wrong reason. "Never seek negative attention for it is shameful! It is never to be applauded nor is it necessary!" The turkey continued to act out in disgust and agreed with Rise's sister. "Now go over there to apologize to the bird to apologize for your rude behavior. I don't know what his mother will do to you but apologize to her!" Other birds stood by of all kinds. The look of shame grew.

Rise did not realize the shame he brought at the expense of rudeness. Rise went to apologize. Then said, "Please may I have a feather from your tail?"

The birds flapped there wings as if they were applauding and with nods of approval. Miss's bird gave his sister a high five! "Be polite!" Rise woke up with a smile while in his deep thoughts.

He woke up and a crowd of bears stood in their tracks!

Rise was resting against the tree and woke up in uniform clothing! "Nice duds," said a baby cub. Rise stood up held his nod downwardly like, "Church," and his walk turn into a trout, that turned into a jog, that turned into a run that turned into flight!

Derondon's parents have been waiting on him to return home. He said bye to his friends and his smile quickly turned into fright. Why the long stares, haven't you seen a happy apple bear before? "Apple Bear this," his aunt and uncle said at the same time. They were pointing at the clock.

"Why yes, Coodie is cool!" said Derondon. "We learned many things today. We are four Musketbears and I'm the new addition. I mean I'm on the slap-box team! We are learning how to defend ourselves when attacked! It's the best day ever!"

Derondon nearly made his way to his room and his surrogate parents said, "We have been thinking and you have been correct about Coodie and his arrogance and controlling behavior!

Why didn't we realize this before but we agree, he's evil! But, but…" said his aunt and uncle! "Coodie took away the things you want. First in everything! First First First! It's time to put a stop to his first-ness!"

The weight on Derondon's face got heavy then his face took a reflection of anger then confusion then anger then angrier until the blood in his eyes returned to green envy! "I will be first," said Derondon. His aunt and uncle knew they could change Derondon back.

Their focus was greed! Nothing would stop their plan of collecting the insurance policy and allowing Derondon to get into trouble that result into his removal so they could travel around the world without him. Derondon passed his aunt and uncle's room and noticed a pistol. He went to further to investigate. It was loaded.

He was curious and picked up the gun. He pointed it into the mirror and his eyes bled the color green! *Kids, whenever you see a gun and you're alone stay far away and don't touch it!*

It was Sunday and Coodie still excited about Rise helping the Musketbears. Coodie remembered to ask his pastor about a scripture to read to strengthen him, turning the other cheek or not and if he let God down by not fasting when he thought he could and failed.

Coodie's pastor was powerful and even more when he preached. His words always touched Coodie's heart and everyone that attends church. He showed his appreciation for all the members that made it and asked with concern for the other members of the church that were unable to attend. He was a gift from God. The church members respected him deeply and many of the members have been part of the church for a long time.

Fire and brimstone with a tone and voice of reason and purpose! With enormous respect and appreciation for his pastor, Coodie humbly asked his questions and his pastor explained the following: "In the book of John, fasting works best by eating a lite breakfast then fasting for lunch, and turning the other cheek has several meanings.

For instance badmouthing, neighbors that treat others unkindly, and aggressive behavior by not engaging with revenge. Coodie appeared relieved but with uncertainty. And yes, Coodie asked the biggest questioned of all! "Should I allow the side of my face to be slapped for a second time?" said Coodie.

His pastor gave him all the answers he needed when he said to pray on it! Coodie did pray on it and many times afterwards. Coodie prayed on the way to school, after school, and before bedtime. Coodie memorized John 14:1-7. Coodie left church feeling revitalized and joyous. Coodie is clumsy and stumbled into Barns who is always seeking trouble. "Oh excuse me," said Coodie. "My bad, I did not see you."

Barns was already in Coodie's path. "I should knock you out!" Barns was a test of Coodies faith.

"God bless you, it was my fault, are you okay?"

"Just watch where you walk!"

"Get in the car, Coodie," said his older brother.

Barns, a former nationally ranked chess champion that also had a reputation as the neighborhood trouble maker by forcing bears out of the neighborhood if they didn't live there. He didn't care if they lived in the neighborhood or not, it was an expression of power.

Barns was influenced by a spell delivered by Romondon that taught him to care only for himself and nobody else, that to have people fear him rather than respect him. Together they owned sections of the area in Bearsville and had intentions of creating another level of the sport and fun to slap boxing!

Every spring picnic basket season, there was always a major "Slap boxing tournament for bears around town. It's a great alternative to overly aggressive and fighting behavior when cubbies can't settle their differences verbally. It was a form of boxing but with open fist. The rules are as follows, one can hit or strike another with open hands any place on the head and face area as hard as they see fit.

Three rounds were the minimal and if the opponent quit before the three rounds, he or she would lose and the boxing is over.

Great friendships were established as an outcome. Hugs and handshakes and no love lost. In fact, bystanders appreciated and recognized the bravery, courage, and honor in settling a disagreement like respectable bears. "Keeps the bears from fighting and it shows leadership and I like that it's over and they laugh about it," said a bystander-bear that witnessed the play-fight firsthand.

Dignity was never lost because of the art, technique, and skills of play-fighting. However, some slap boxers from the underground like Barns and Romondon believed it was a way to control the streets! The underground bully bears were on high alert for recruitment of potential slap boxers by any means necessary!

When he returned home that Sunday afternoon, Coodie told his mother about fasting and she said the exact same thing his pastor suggested.

Coodie fasted the following day and God was not angry for him missing the first time fasting. "Church is good, God is good all the time! Boo!" Yes it's Menzy the other musketeer.

"Catch and block any flies, Coodie?" asked Menzy.

"No, anybody else?" asked Coodie. "Nobody caught any flies?"

They all said, "Where's Rise?"

"Somebody call me? Ahhhh!" The three Musketbears nearly jumped out of their seats! Of course Rise was with the Musketbears the entire way! He was concerned that time was getting near for Romondon to complete his evil wrath of destruction on the bears! "It is time to go to the next level," said Rise. "Follow me!"

The Musketbears plus one headed to the river of fish! "Rise you seem smart, so can I ask you a question?" asked Gina. "How do you let someone know that you like them but they don't know anything about it?"

Menzy came over to eavesdrop. "Get away, Menzy! I'm trying to ask Rise a question!" said Gina emphatically.

"Ah-ha you like Coodie, don't you?" asked Menzy.

Gina chased Menzy around the park and back again as Menzy screamed for his life. As they circled several times, Derondon took advantage of the series of questions by asking a few of his own. "Will life get better or worse when we grow up?" said Derondon. Rise told Derondon the life was supposed to get better.

"Supposed to?"

"What do you mean by that? Life can be what you make of it. One can choose to do the right thing even when things go wrong. How can you do the right thing when others are telling you the wrong thing is right?" Derondon explained further. "My parents are in the hospital because of a car accident. When they come out, they don't want me. I don't understand. My aunt and uncle talk about how bad things are today and with my friends I feel alone."

At that point of the conversation, Rise heard the voice of his sister and said, "The friends that speak of goodwill and read the Bible are good friends. A friend that speaks from his heart is a good friend. You are a leader of the bears. Just look at friends that respect you only.

God loves us all. Trust him when man fails. You have the support of angles that will listen to your heart. God will never let you down. He forgives you. Let not your heart be troubled, son."

"Is it because they can't take care of me? Or did I do something wrong. I do want to be a leader. I'm always a follower. I can do many things as good as anyone else. Can you tell me why things are so confusing?! It is better to do right when even if it makes you not popular because in the end what is right stays right! I want to make a difference in the world but how?"

"Kindness is a good start."

Coodie came over as he could not help from overhearing the conversation.

"My pastor at my church gave me a scripture. After learning the verses and memorizing it, I returned to him and told him that I thought the scripture was helpful. I asked him if he would give me another scripture. He told me to continue reading that same scripture. At first I felt he did not believe that I memorized it but ever though I did, I followed what he told me.

I felt silly because I knew it but sometimes it's not what you can remember, it's what you remember to tell others. Sometimes it hard to be kind, especially when bears around you are not."

"How do I get others to be kind?"

"Look here at the animals. See how they get along. They share their space and they work together. Point out that which is good and make friends with others of that which is good. It is a practice indeed and practice makes perfect." After the Musketbears arrived to the lake of fish and Gina completed her chase with Menzy, they focused their attention on Rise.

Rise reviewed the ballet dance, shoo fly, and Please Sir May I Have a Feather from Your Tail techniques. "You are ready take the fish out of the water! I watched my dad do this, look out!" said Menzy. Menzy went into the water and with one foot in front of the other facing against the current slipped off a slippery rock into the water face forward and a fish swam right into his mouth.

"Maybe you should keep legs open and you mouth close young apprentice!" The other Musketbears laughed but little did they know it was time for them take a dab at it themselves.

One by one and two by two, they all found balance a difficult task. After twenty minutes, it became evident that none of the Musketbears practiced. It is better we practice balance on land before sea. The team young apprentices lived up to their name. *Practice makes perfect and if you listen you will succeed. If you do no homework, your success is at risk.* Everyone came close to the river to see their reflection.

Rise went into the river stream section of the lake to study the behavior of their fish to seek its image beyond the illusion. "As you look into the water, you can see the reflections of nature, a mirror image of yourself, then the water, and lastly the fish. The fish creates the illusion to hide its image to prevent your purpose to catch the fish. To catch the fish, look beyond the illusion the water has created out of the fish, then you will see the fish for what it is, and that is dinner!"

Rise caught a fish with one attempt while explaining at the same time! The apple bears were ecstatic and leaped for joy! Their confidence was restored! Practice went to another level. Rise encouraged the apple bear cat kids to work in groups and in partners. He would talk with his apprentices in a circle with himself in the middle. He reminded them that the defending is simply defending and not to be offending. The Musketbears were to be humble and respectful as leaders.

He reviewed ways to keep focus and benefits of how hard work make perfection. "Respect all that you confront, for there is good in us all, even in combat," said Rise.

Other bears from the park stopped, stared, and a sense of pride roamed the area. Big bears can learn what's good in the hearts of little bears because big bears made little bears believe in what is good.

"The reflection of tradition and honor for generations from the good stuff is learning what becomes beautiful. When the learning from big bears becomes unattractive it breeds confusion, shame, and resentment," said Rise. Rise picked up a rock and had each apple bear catch it one by one. Then Rise instructed the bears to stand under a tree.

Of course, Menzy want to go first without a clue of what was yet to come. "Can I go first?" asked Menzy. Rise tossed the rock over the tree that was filled with leaves. Menzy lost sight of the rock and it hit square on the top of his head. The group became amused.

Rise told Menzy, "The beauty of trees had more than shape and space as a responsibility. It direct winds, releases oxygen for us to breathe, provides protection for us and other animals, food, and warning of dangerous weather. Menzy, I will toss the same rock but this time close your eyes and consider other senses and tell me what you have learned."

"To duck, it frightened me because I could hear the rock breaking through leaves before it lands," said Menzy.

"Very good," said Rise.

"Why is that good I became more afraid?"

"Remember, Menzy, fear is an emotion until knowledge and understanding is applied." Like the Bible says, "Let not your heart be troubled."

"Menzy, this time catch the rock with what you have learned." Menzy watched the rock leave Rise's hand and followed its path through the leaves and his energy motivated him to track what he heard to predict the rock's location. Menzy caught the rock! The Musketbears leaped for joy!

"Come here Derondon and stand by the tree."

Derondon left the circle and did as instructed.

Rise picked up a pebble and tossed it at Derondon. Derondon stood there as the pebble hit him on his chest. Menzy laughed because he can't help himself.

"What? He laughed at me," said Menzy.

"This time, Menzy, watch the path of the rock as it leaves my hand," said Rise.

Derondon had plenty of time to move out of the way.

"What have you learned, Menzy? That even a small rock hurts!" The Musketbears laughed. "Life is full of small rocks. Your job is to get out of the way! Coodie, come here," Rise said.

Rise picked up a hand full of pebbles and tossed them at Coodie. Coodie stood there as multiple rocks hit him everywhere. "Why didn't he do anything?" asked Derondon.

Rise asked Derondon to come in his place. Rise tossed a hand full of pebbles at Derondon and he did the same. Rise asked Derondon to become a leader and grabbed a hand full of pebbles at Derondon but this time

Derondon ducked and protected himself. The Musketbears were puzzled about the exercise. "So what, who was right?" they asked.

Rise said, "It is better to do something to lead rather than do nothing at all."

"My head hurts," said Gina.

"I got it," said Coodie. "We all can be leaders if we do something but if we do nothing, we become followers. It's a practice like most things." Derondon began to understand and he began to realize the value of friendship and the roles we have until we choose to make a difference. Derondon began to cry and his group gave him a hug.

Rise told the Musketbears to practice. Two days away from the slap-boxing tournament. Little did the Musketbears know that out of the crowd of watchers were several bully-boys from school. They saw Derondon, who had been missing from the crew.

Coodie, Menzy, and Gina was unware still that it was Derondon that slapped Coodie that day on the sand lot near the ware house while the apple bears built the scooter.

The Musketbears were heading home. "Goodbye, Rise" the Musketbears said. The Musketbears's confidence grew greatly. All the way home the practiced the various techniques. Derondon asked Menzy to toss a rock at him for practice. Derondon went to get a rock and saw that they were being followed by his former group of bully boys. Derondon returned back to group. "Where is the rock?" asked Menzy.

"Never mind," yelled Derondon. Derondon startled the group.

"Everyting okay?" asked Gina.

"I'm fine," said Derondon. Yes Coodie heard Derondon say the word "fine." Coodie did not question Derondon's statement and kept the thought of why Derondon's direction to reflect on another time.

Everyone made it home safely from the park and said goodbye. Derondon had just walked into his door and seconds later he hear a knock on his door. He knew who it was. Do you care to guess?

Derondon hesitated to answer but he knew who was at the door. "Excuse me sir may we have a feather from your tail?" as the bully boys laughed loudly. "What are you up to?" said one of the bully boys.

"You do plan to join us in the slap-boxing tournament at school with us, right?" said Barns. Barns was one of the bully boy rulers! Barns had a reputation for being a troublemaker, instigator, and was notorious for setting up apple bears to fight each other. Barns rarely attended school and when he went, danger and acts of violence were sure to follow. "You missed two meetings.

What happened to you? Did you get into a picnic basket and got all yummy and stuff!" Derondon's aunt and uncle hid in the kitchen to listen the little bears' conversation.

Derondon's aunt and uncle chose to do nothing to keep Derondon in his place as being a troublesome bear that would eventually be taken away to cubby protections unit! "No, everything is cool. I wanted to know how they plan to win against us and had to make them think I roll with them."

The timing was awful for poor Derondon. It seemed like he was trying to turn a new leaf and something kept pulling him back in. Or was Derondon finally going to get the revenge he had been seeking?

Peer pressure is as tough as you make it. Doing something is better than doing nothing. It's much easier to avoid trouble sooner than later than to allow it to grow much too deep to swim out of. Just know you will know who your real friends are when you don't agree with them more than agreeing with them. Choosing to not engage with troublemakers early and you may be saving another peer from making the same mistake too. Just know if you get in too deep you can talk to someone that have a history of doing the right thing and he or she doesn't have to be a relative. Counselors, teachers, authorities, security, preachers and church members are a good choice.

CHAPTER TWELVE

"Okay Derondon, just checkin' wit-chu! I can't stand the crack-head sellouts, see you in school tomorrow," said Barns. A regular day started at school but how was it going to end? Coodie woke up early to practice. "Mom, the phone!" *Ring, ring, ring*! Coodie made an announcement before it rang! His mother was making porridge. She leaves the stove while the porridge is coming and has a bad feeling that it was the same person calling—agents! "Coodie! How did you know the phone would ring?"

"Oh, it rings every day at this time."

"You wasn't looking at the clock!"

"Oh. Just a guess."

Fearfully, she reached for the phone! "Hello? Hello!" She was frustrated with the amount of phone calls every day and all the time. On his way out, he could see in the corners of his eyes his mother's reaction to the phone call. She appeared frightened.

Rise watched him in the process. "I see he is improving daily," said Juan Tracy. "Yes, and I feel my sister's presence each training session. Coodie might direct us there to where my sister is after all. He is learning faster than the others— fascinating! Coodie did his morning readings, inspiring self-talks, and prayers that he not have problems on his way to school and back."

Coodie had a reputation and didn't know it. Holding doors before school, after school, at lunch time for his classmates, greeting the teachers, and assisting the school assistant principal with petty inappropriate behavior was out of the kindness of his heart and his gratitude for attending the school in a neighbor that his friends from the old neighborhood made him feel good even when he could not see them until lunch time or after school.

Coodie passed out plastic forks and spoons before he ate to further greet his classmates or provide a warning when the school principal was coming to speak to the all of his classmates. When it was time for assemblies, Coodie bear was off to the races to let classes know even though it was announced on the speaker system. Fights did break out and Coodie bear would share how important it was to work together and as a result, fewer and fewer fights occurred.

We should not fight in school. Imagine classrooms in schools assigning a weekly supporter of three students, a planner of activities, hostess, and talent show manager to organize shows in the auditorium that simply sits there unoccupied. Students from middle school do have the capability to take ownership and independently handle the responsibilities. We should not fight at all. Talk with each other to settle it out.

Coodie often made it a habit to thank his classmates for trusting that it was because he cares. Coodie believed his teachers, classmates, and staff were the best in town. "We are competing against other schools with our education and learning. Imagine how well they are doing," Coodie often said.

He wanted all the bears to be successful or have a fighting chance at success!

Coodie surrounded himself with classmates that wanted the best out of each other to succeed. Coodie often daydreamed during his downtime of completing his schoolwork assignments in class. He missed many of his favorite teachers and drama did follow in some of his classes. His teacher, Mr. G and other teachers were award-winning supporters of education, but at the hands incidental contact others that led us to question their commitment to excellence.

Coodie's daydreaming
reflections

Coodie Bear's special powers produced intellect and sight by design. Coodie Bear was taken to a birthday party by age six. He had never won anything before. A game of Pin The Tail On The Donkey began the moment he arrived and the prize included an air rocket! Coodie Bear learned of the prize and did not hesitate to participate. "In the back of the line!" said the grownups. Coodie Bear was anxious.

Coodie Bear had recalled a Saturday morning cartoon of how imagining objects of looking an object such an airplane for long periods stays in the memory like a picture for long periods! "That's it—I will stare at the donkey's tail to win," said Coodie to himself. I could just stare at something long enough it would stay in his mind as an image. Coodie bear's confidence soared!

Two minutes in his excitement he thought to himself that it would be unfair if he knew how to win and if his peers were unaware of his idea and decided to share with anyone around him. Coodie's kindness extended beyond and understood how sharing is caring. He told the other bears to stare at the donkey's backside for long periods and see the image in your mind to win.

"Try it. Look at something in your room and count for ten seconds then close your eyes to see if you can see the image… Good job!" Coodie's peers did not seem interested in his idea so he wished them "Good luck!"

Coodie Bear could barely stand still in line out of excitement! One the adult bears asked, "Why are you so excited and anxious?"

Coodie Bear told of his discovery of sight and the idea of winning a rocket set was a prize he wished for. "I've seen the very same rocket set on Saturday mornings while watching my favorite cartoons on TV," said Coodie. His turn came. Coodie was so anxious he forgot to stare the last minute thinking he had more time.

There were many other bears that gathered to see if Coodie Bear was right at winning. Coodie could sense that not everyone had the same excitement as he did and he was right. Just like having friends, some friends are happy that you for you to win and some friends are not happy.

Sportsmanship is a great way to get along with others and show support. Your day will come to win something and by thinking that way, it keeps your spirits up. Pats on the back, a smile or saying, "Good Job!" comes back to you one day too and it makes the world go round.

Coodie Bear's eyes were covered unexpectedly by the blindfolds; it scared him and sent his heart rate up but he began to breathe deeply and steady to keep calm! Adult bears spun Coodie Bear around and around several times to distort the sense of direction. Coodie began to settle his thoughts and asked, "I am in front of the donkey?"

The group grew larger. Whispers and laughter increased and doubt entered Coodie bear's mind. "Yes," said one of the grownup bears. Coodie was steady and found his sense of sight and imagined the donkey's backside just like he explained to his peer-bears. He stuck the pin on the right place of the donkey's backside and a huge roar of excitement shocked Coodie.

He won! The air rocket was handed to him and it was an exciting day for Coodie. When the party ended, Coodie took the air rocket out to play and shared the activity with his peer-bears.

Coodie Bear loved school. In the fourth grade, it was time to take the national tests that were held at all schools across Bearsville! Coodie was thrilled to complete all parts to the test. The test was like letting the teacher know everything you have learned in school.

Coodie overheard that teachers brought treats, games, and prizes from their own bank account to pay for it! He appreciated his teacher for bringing games and magnets to school for the class to play with when work was completed. He would inform his teacher that he would make them proud of him by getting all answers on the test as best as he could because he appreciated them greatly for being kind.

In Coodie's mind he believed that if he listened to his teacher and did a good job, she would stay. Coodie did his best to get all questions correct on the national test. Coodie asked every few days if his teacher for the test results so that his teacher would be happy to see how well he thought he did. When the test returned, his teacher was excited for Coodie. His test results were very good and he had top national rankings! The teacher shared ice cream with the class!

Finally, the family made it home to their new neighborhood. The neighbors were friendly. Coodie helped to move furniture to the new home.

He was clumsy, however, as he accidently dropped the lamp on to the ground and it broke. His mother said, "That old lamp needed to be replaced anyways, don't worry. I'll clean that up after were are moved in."

Coodie loved his mother and he told her so. That night, he washed his mother's feet while his mother explained that his first day of school was tomorrow and for him to not have trouble with his teachers. Coodie responded by sharing that he knew that having a family this large was enough to worry about and that day he told his mother, "You will never have any trouble from me."

His mother came to tears. He asked his mother why she was crying and his mother said, "No reason. These are happy tears."

Within the same minute, the phone rang. Coodie's mother answered the phone but was visibly shaken by the ring. She said under her breath, "Who's calling this time of day?" When she answered the phone, the caller hung up.

Ten minutes later, the phone rang again and the same thing happened. The phone rang in several times that night. When Coodie's other sibling bears came to her aid, everyone was in the room got quiet. Coodie asked, "Why so quiet?" and everyone gave a different response at the same time. Coodie went to bed and chose to forget the entire event. It was natural to not understand everything that was going on at home. Big words would have meaning in time. If it was important, trust that big bears will make the time to explain.

A room full of girls! Coodie believed in his schoolmates and supported the administrators. Between class time and heading to the next class, Coodie guarded the hallways, encouraging and complimenting acts of kindness. He made friends very easily. He would stop in a classroom unannounced and ask the teacher if he could be of assistance. The administrator got so busy dealing with students and allowed Coodie to talk with students that had social conflicts. Coodie had a favorite saying: "Why are you wasting your time on your school mate arguing when one day you will need their assistance?" or "The first one that laughs is the smartest," or "This technique worked better with the girls!" Coodie believed humor was the answer to all conflict. Coodie walked into one class and it was only girls.

Coodie shook in his feet and nearly stumbled in the classroom for inspection of compliance and wanted the new students to get off on the right bear foot. To save himself from being embarrassed, he kept his focus and asked his teacher if he could remind the new students to not hang out in the hallways to avoid stranger danger.

The classroom had girls with flirting eyes! It made Coodie extra nervous because he had his shy moments and always knew to never show interest in one girl to cause jealousy of another so he avoided girls altogether. The discussion of being carful from stranger danger suddenly became a stage! The teacher was very pretty and that was enough pressure.

A student seemed to detect Coodie's shy sensors intensifying and asked, "What kind of danger should we look for?"

The floor did become a stage to the girls in class and shyness was taking over! Nothing came out of the mouth of teacher and everything became slow motion. Coodie said, "You have bad girls in your class, they know stranger danger and what it looks like!"

A student went further and said, "Well show us what they will do!"

Coodie was too far to run and if he did, he would lose all the nerve he had thus far to encourage and compliment students he met. Coodie began sweating and the girls stared! "Mrs. Jones, you have bad students in this class. Please talk to them."

Mrs. Jones asked the class to be quiet and for Coodie to explain further. Coodie did the first two minutes of Michael Jackson's "Billie Jean!" The giggles and smiles spread like the bestselling cologne entered the room.

Coodie was never more embarrassed and left the room! That class would never live it down and asked Coodie to explain more. Coodie was determined to encourage each class to work hard and promised to return if the class continued working on completing all assignments and didn't give Mrs. Jones any problems.

Coodie got a report of good behavior every week for the entire school year. A student came to meet with him and Coodie made every goal of complaint work down to every detail. Every time Coodie walked past the classroom, he could hear a roar of screams. Coodie knew he was never going in the classroom ever again!

At lunchtime, the girls were responsible to sit on one side and the boys on the other. Coodie rarely looked at girls and after his experience, he never looked back. During situations of conflict between girls, Coodie would remind the class that other schools are working harder than us and if we let the teacher teach then we can work harder than them and one day get a job because our success.

CHAPTER THIRTEEN

One week later, Coodie's teacher was very tearful as she had bad news. She regretted to inform Coodie that it was impossible to score that high with top honors of 5 percent in the area where Coodie lived and the test needed to be retaken. Coodie was crushed that it hurt his teacher's feelings and his.

The energy left the classroom and retaking the test and losing recess as punishment further felt impossible. Coodie asked his teacher if she would remain as his teacher if he did not do well and his teacher said yes and it was good enough for him.

However, Coodie's teacher suddenly became ill and a substitute replaced her for the remainder of the school year. The substitute teacher was a former military serviceman and his idea of instructions was far different from the regular teacher. In fact he had a paddle for any student that was over talkative. One student that talked back was brought to the front of the class and was paddled several times over.

The student danced away but each time he tried to get away the teacher held him back down. The entire class went into shock! At lunchtime, the bears gathered in a meeting to question if the substitute was correct for what he was doing toward to bears.

They decided to let the teacher know, "We are good apple bears and we never received punishments like this and we do not deserve it now!" Just then, the student that received a paddle returned back to class because he was angry and the second he was let go, he ran out of the classroom. He was thinking of never returning back to school ever again at lunch.

The class shared the good news and informed the battered bear he had no more worries. They told the battered bear that other teachers were informed of his mistreatment and he would get fired, except we did know for sure. "After all, it was wrong and we did our part to stop it."

The battered bear said, "Great. His paddle is still here and so are his other things!" Not sure what went on in the battered bear's mind but one answer was revenge! First, he tucked the paddle in his pants but was too large to hide successfully. Second, he went to hide the paddle inside a desk but was fearful the teacher might find to paddle. Suddenly it dawned on him to toss the paddle out of the window! He opened the window and *swoosh, splash* went the paddle! "Nobody tell him what happened and it will be over!" Half the class warned him not to do anything but his revenge was to ensure it would not happen to any other bears!

"Will anybody tell if I threw it out the window?" he asked. Nobody said yes.

The teacher returned to gather his things. He noticed that the bear he paddled had returned. "I see you made it back to school!" He was impressed that the class was quiet.

Rumor had it, the battered bear's mother called the school to complain to the principal about paddling students as a form of corporal punishment! The teacher said, "Your little ass deserved a paddle!" and the battered bear said, "Your ass shouldn't paddle apple bear kids."

At the class, the teacher screamed, "Where is my paddle! When I find out, all of you will get a paddle!" One of the bears said, "You can't do that!" and one of the bears ran out of the classroom to get help.

The teacher threatened the entire class again and the battered bear spoke up like a hero and said, "I threw the paddle out of the window!"

The teacher looked concerned. He may have denied having a paddle at all! The teacher walked toward the window to search for the paddle. He opened the window and saw paddle four stories below smashed into pieces. The teacher went straight towards the battered warrior in a threatening manner and seconds before he got there, two teachers and the other hero bear that left earlier get help rushed in with an angry tone, "What's happening here?!"

The battered bear and his sidekick saved the day as heroes! He was right, he didn't deserve a paddle and getting help by telling someone was better than allowing the wrong to get away! Speaking of heroes, Mr.G gave the class a lot to smile about. He encouraged them to believe in themselves! Here's how: His name is Mr.G. Mr. G never allowed any disruptions in his classroom. Mr. G was a no-nonsense kind of teacher with an undying desire to ensure his students were educated and made each lesson related to survival skills and with a belief system of building our confidence and knowledge of how to own a business.

His favorite sayings was "absolute silence please!" He always negotiated the class to work first and have social time when work was done. That was fair! His class was fun. He was fun because he never talked down on his students. He passed out tickets for the bears that worked the hardest and had drawings several times during one class period.

He never sat down until we took a test. He cared and he would also say, "You came to school and I appreciate you for that, so learn something new."

One day for science, our project was to build a rocket! Yes a rocket! We practiced often and understood what made things go by use of rocket power.

After much practice and test flights, it was time to unleash the granddaddy of rockets!

The rocket could propel 1,500 feet! We were required to call the airport nearby to get the permission to shoot our rocket! An announcement went out to invite the school to witness the rocket blast off! A very large crowd attended. The class walked of the distance of 15 hundred feet from the audience. We set the rocket into action.

It was a wondrous sight as the rocket began its descent. It went straight to its final landing destination which was right in front of the audience. The crowd of apple bears cheered. They were very proud.

In Coodie's homeroom, his teacher, Mr. Smith had a good heart and had played a listening game in all of his classes for over a decade! He told the class, "The last student that talks after the third bell will receive a paddle in front of the class with your permission and from your parents!"

Coodie asked a peer, "What did he just say? Is this true about what he just said that he plans to do Menzy?"

"Are students receiving paddles for talking?" Menzy whispered.

"Shhh yes and he hits very hard on the fanny!"

"I heard about him before we got here, he's mean," said Menzy.

Coodie explained to Menzy, "Who is giving the permission?" Menzy replied, "Everyone is getting paddled so be quiet! The first bell just rang!"

Coodie said to Menzy, "Did you ever get a paddle before?"

Menzy replied, "Yes and it hurt too! So be quiet before the second bell rings!"

Coodie was puzzled even further. Coodie heard the second and the third bell and was extra quiet to see how it goes! When the third bell rang, several students struggled to get quiet immediately and the last student talking was discovered by the class of students. They'd screamed and point.

"Come down and get the paddle, it was you!'

The class laughed at the last apple bear for being talking! *Whack*! Went the paddle. Embarrassment followed by "Next time, it won't be me!" Coodie was taken by routine of events and told Menzy to pass the word that paddling was only given by permission by you! Menzy did relay the message to several students.

Coodie struggled with the idea that has classmates with amazing hearts and full of joy would agree with the deception and mistreatment. Coodie knew his time could happen and will let his hero powers kick in! And sooner than later it happened!

"Coodie did it! He was last! That's right it was him!"

"Okay Coodie Bear, bring it on down and come get, "da-paddle!" The class was even more taken back by the interaction between teacher and the classmates let out a wave of loud outburst similar to that of a prize fight "Oh this is going to be good!" Coodie stood up out of his seat, walked in the direction of his teacher, and began to turn around.

His teacher had the attitude of an executioner as he picked up the paddle and waved it around like he had a club with nails! Coodie's voice and tone was like that of a self-proclaimed game show host calling himself to the stage, "I'm coming and I'm turning around!"

The class nearly rose to their feet and would have if the wasn't afraid. Let the game show begin! Coodie wanted his voice and volume loud and clear. Coodie's confidence grew and felt the need to emphasis a playful side to encourage his classmates to become active listeners!

His teacher began to wind up with his paddle once more simulating a batter in the batter's box to over-emphasize the inevitable would surely come one way or another before Coodie got into position. Coodie got within striking distance. Just before he could turn into position Coodie said, "Ah-ah- ahhh!".. "No you won't!"

His teacher laughed and said, "Turn around for the paddle apple-bear!"

Coodie said again, "Ah ahh ahh. No you don't! And you can't."

His teacher said, "why not?" I can paddle you! "It was you who was talking last!"

Coodie said, "I haven't given you permission and my momma bear sure didn't either!"

By then, the teacher's face was on its way to reality of consciousness! He cracked an unwelcomed smile on his face. He nearly look puzzled!

He stated to the class that he had been paddling the bears for over sixteen seasons and this day, it ended! The look on the students' face was as if they witnessed the crack in the Liberty Bell that appeared right before their eyes! Coodie cracked a sixteen year code to paddling apple bears! But the reaction was so stunning, the class was frozen! More than half of them said, "What happened? Why did you not give Coodie a paddle?"

Coodie said that it was because he didn't give permission and that everyone always had the power to say no!

Then half the class, still stunned, said, "What should we do?" Coodie told the class he had saved their hides and that it was their duty to speak up! More students asked what they could do. Coodie said, "You need to tell someone what happened today and before you tell them, demand that they tell ten people about what happened today and how important it is to listen to what's happening to them around town and the newspapers because a paddle could come to them if they don't listen! Pay Attention! The students began to breathe again. One student asked, "What if they don't believe us?"

Coodie said, "They will!"

Derondon went to bed in a world-wind of confusion, pain, and anger. He on one hand finally learned what friendships were made of. He understood what was missing in his young cubby's life of loneliness. He could describe what kindness looked like and how to practice it with others. After many disappointments and attempts to become a leader, Derondon could recall times when he demonstrated leadership qualities.

Derondon's surrogate parents took him to attend activities and events for the purpose of following Coodie. His mother and father were admirers or Coodie and appreciated Coodies's kindness.

They grew up together. Derondon's reflections since Coodie was six months old, he imagined being there from conversations on the phone. Little league. Derondon's revelation made him fall into a deep sleep of reflection. His dream became a world wind of compassion of reality! Here's how:

Derondon was sitting with his mother in the waiting room to get his vaccinations to start kindergarten. His mother said hello to Coodie's mother in the room of fearful needle land. The nurse walked around the room with a huge needle and the look of terror that set him and other potentials on fire to become more afraid than before. The nurse said, "Pain is part of the process. It's natural to cry!" Romondon was on the lookout for Coodie and knew he could find him in his dreams.

On his way, he could detect terror of dreams. He became compelled to investigate. It was Derondon having a bad dream. Then it hit Romondon to get the bully boys to turn Derondon gangster immediately!

Romondon fled. Derondon's dream continued to spiral into his past. Derondon's mother observed Coodie receiving a needle, but did not cry. Derondon's mother became amazed by the bravery that Coodie possessed. Coodie and his mother went into the other room.

It was Derondon's turn for his injection of pain! A different nurse who was a male nurse come to give Derondon his injection to apply the first safe injection that reduced pain. Derondon's reaction to the injection reduced his fear and it was far less painful. The energy in the room became a ray of sunshine and kindness.

The nurse was escorted out by the other nurses. If you guessed that it was his aunt! You are right! From Coodie and his mother's perspective, it went down in this order. At age five, Coodie witnessed a fearful scene. He and other apple-bear cat kids were preparing for kindergarten and had to get required vaccinations to prevent the spread various diseases in school.

CHAPTER FOURTEEN

Coodie and his mother could hear young apple bear cat kids crying from the painful needle injections delivered by the nurse. "Bang! Right into the arm! No worries, next! Just part of the process!" and he heard, "It's natural for them to cry!" Coodie didn't believe that grabbing apple bear cat kids and snatching them away and aggressively stabbing the giant needle was necessary! Observing the scene, Coodie applied his superpowers!

Coodie told his mother, "Mom, if you hold me I won't cry!" His mother fell to tears and agreed. When his turn came, Coodie's entire body shook but he did not cry! The nurse was astounded! She even rattled that needle a bit deeper! And Coodie shook some more. The nurse said it was common for the Apple Bears to cry and that after so many years, "this one is the first to not cry!"

The nurse was disappointed and Coodie's momma began to cry even more. Coodie bear politely asked his mother if he could ask the nurse a question.

Coodie asked the nurse if the skin had holes. The nurse thought for a second and said, "Yes!"

Coodie Bear said, "You are choosing the wrong hole."

The nurse said, "What do you mean?"

"Because there are many holes so the needle should go straight in! You may need to open the skin to get to the right hole!" The nurse went to get a male nurse. He returned after experimenting with administering the needle as instructed. The nurse returned and asked for Coodie's name. He stated that he wanted to name the discovery after Coodie. Coodie's mother was hesitant and did just dat! Taaddaaah!

Could the attention that continually showed up present itself as an effect on Coodie's mother to become fearful of Coodie's mystical powers? Why was his mother reluctant to say Coodie's name if somebody was watching her? Did she believe it's witchcraft, that Coodie posse? If you guessed that it was Derondon's aunt that gave injections that fearful day, you are right!

Derondon woke up out of his dream state with the image of Coodie leaving the nurse's office and his aunt being dragged out of the room because she was fired. His aunt's sadness and anger was written on her face.

The nice male nurse applied an injection instead of Derondon's aunt.

His mother appearing happy about Coodie the bear went to thank Coodie's mother for the safe injection! Derondon didn't realize he was the first to receive a proper injection. Derondon woke up a second time in his dream state of dreamland with the sight of Coodie's smile!

School was in session and Derondon came flying down the stairs, late for school with red in his eyes circled with green. Derondon skipped his favorite breakfast of porridge and raced to school. Rumors had a way of getting to school before things develop. The bully boys were at their corner post waiting for Derondon. "Here he comes now," said Barns.

Now it was Barns, a gang of bully-boys and Derondon with red and green eyes leading the gang to school. The clouds had an unusual color that day. It began to chance into purple and grey. Romondon had created destruction in other parts of the continent and began to make its way to town! Winds and the sense of madness, terror, and fear became thick; you could feel it and smell it.

Rise heard Coodie say his prayers, "God thank you for another day. May I get to school and back with no problems and please protect everyone including my family and friends."

Rise could sense danger coming. Rise watched Coodie practice yesterday all that he learned. Coodie practiced throwing rocks into trees to detect it path with success. Coodie practiced detecting the intentions of a fly by blocking the image and destroying the enemy. Coodie practiced respect for his enemy with pleasant communication by not reacting first!

"Rise! Rise! Rise! RISE, ARE YOU THERE?" It was Juan-Tracy calling on Rise and nearly fearful that he couldn't be heard by Rise. It was silent… Coodie was heading toward

Derondon, Barns, and the bully boys! Derondon saw Coodie looking up to God. Derondon put his mask on and so did the bully boys. Derondon checked his weapon, tucked it deeper inside his clothing and told Barns, "handle it!" "Checkmate! Here comes church boy Coodie movin-this way as planned!" Coodie turned the corner, and the Bully-boys interrupted Coodie's passing.

Barns stood in front as the bully boys that were three now became seven! "We know you belong to a gang and we know you are not from around here," said Barns "Church boy! I know you too and you already know I live near you," said Coodie. The bully boys began to circle Coodie. Rise above, wanted to intervene. His energy and confidence are equal to his task of protection of Coodie.

Rise's wings are visible for the first time. Rise's wings of spiritual energy stimulated Coodie's pupils. Coodie's senses and participation are heightened but are unwanted and is visibly undesired. Coodie is realizing his assertion of words must end with exclamation marks of defense!

Coodie spoke to Barns and knew his intentions at the same time were not of peace. He already planned to have war with Coodie and so Coodie's thought to turn the other cheek was no more! With focus, calm and stimulated pupils Coodie accepts and bought time and seconds allowed while the Bully-Boys circles him.

He knew his greatest heroes, God and his teacher, were there. If he backed down, it would not stop. Running was not an option. Coodie began counting the bully boys that began surrounding him. He didn't want Barns to know he was counting, so with his peripheral vision, he kept his eye on Barns and began counting, predicting the motion, anticipating the point of attack, and transitioned from uncertainty into certainty by participating in a play.

It became a dance! Coodie is ready yet serious. Barns signaled the attack with his face and eyes! "His eyes!" Yes, his eyes, says Coodie to himself. Coodie participated. Coodie put his arms out to anticipate a take down, and two bully boys went for it!

Right before the two bully-boys reached for his arms while Coodie continued looking forward, he bent his arms and threw his elbow into the gut of Bully Boy One and Bully Boy Two. Anticipating a kick by Bully Boy Three, Coodie stepped forward and shifted two his right.

The bully boy fell forward and Coodie used his balance against him as he fell into a left cross. Coodie began to make eye contact with Barns. Barns' eye became a navigator of each attack. Bully Boys Four and Five slowed down their attack. Coodie never turned around and read Barns' eyes for detection of attacks. Barns sent attackers Four and Five.

Before they could make a blow toward Coodie, Attacker Four was punched in the face and knocked unconscious on Coodie's right with a left cross and on Coodie's right, the attacker hopped on Coodie's back and was flipped to the ground.

Attacker Six crept up slowly to apply a chokehold in which Coodie stepped to the exit and released the hold and held the wrist down and threw a left cross knocking him unconscious.

Would-be Attacker Seven stood in distance. Barns had a look of shock on his face and was frozen by the display of the dance. Coodie became alarmed about his friends. He went to his homeroom to look in on his friends. Coodie was late and did not hear the first bell of his homeroom.

Coodie saw Menzy and was relieved. Gina stepped in the classroom ten seconds before the second bell. Coodie was relieved. Coodie began explaining to Menzy that he was attacked by the bully boys wearing masks and his concerned about Musketbears number three, Derondon. Derondon! Where is Derondon, has anyone seen Derondon!?

Fearing he was the next victim to attack, Menzy huddles with Coodie and Gina, "I heard that Derondon is angry and he's beating up apple bears and got into an argument with his homeroom teacher!"

He left the school, saying he would be back! You know what that means when somebody says they will be back? *Ding*! The third bell rang and that was when Coodie was sent down to get the paddle. "Got-cha'll, don't I!"

Coodie asked to use the restroom and then he raced to find Derondon. Students began to fill the hallways with apple bears heading to the next class and noticed that some apple bears were running, scrambling, scattering, and darting wildly out of the classroom and into the direction of Coodie, Menzy and Gina!.

The increase of bears running was near the back of the hallway where Derondon's homeroom was located. They stopped one of Derondon's classmates running in their direction and stopped him on his path.

Where is Derondon! The apple bear's eyes widen with fear. He's in there with a weapon! He's arguing with his teacher! "Mr.G! Mr.G?" said Coodie. "Weapon! Yeah, weapon!"

Not what Coodie imagined he would hear? Coodie believed that Derondon was attacked by the bully boys and that he would help. Seconds flew by. Menzy and Gina caught up with Coodie's racing disbelief and darting dismay propels him in a flighty state of mind.

"What's going on? Is Derondon okay?" asked Gina. In a world-wind of confusion, Coodie raced to Derondon's classroom. Coodie began to disbelieve his thinking. Was Derondon's heart in the right place?

Did his heart turn cold again? Coodie knew he had a temper and was clearly misunderstood.

Each step drew Coodie to feel everything about the essence of being a friend and having faith, trust, and honor began touching his heart. His favorite teacher was under attack by his fellow Musketbears. Students afraid to move as they hid under desks, and behind corners of the classroom fearful of their safety.

A Musketbear who he knew had a load of misconception, misunderstanding, mistreatment, and was misguided by everyone he thought he could trust! The room became a room of disbelief. In the room stood several apple bears appearing trapped against the walls frozen by the confrontation.

Derondon held a deadly slingshot pointed at Mr.G!

Mr.G told Derondon he is wrong for punching a student in his classroom and told Derondon he would amount to nothing. "Mr. G, please don't say anything to Derondon. Derondon, don't do it." Mr.G told Derondon that he is afraid the he would shoot. Derondon pulled back the bands and aimed closer.

"I dare you to think I won't do it."

Coodie moved closer into the aim of fire. "Mr. G! Don't say another word. You are wrong for talking to my friend DAT way! He is my friend and he will always be my friend. If you believe he is wrong, okay but Derondon is holding a weapon at you. You don't know what Derondon is going through and you know nothing about him.

He is my neighbor and he is our friend. Derondon, Mr.G is not going to let you get into any more trouble. You are angry and you have a choice, Derondon, and what you do now will change everything. Please, Derondon, don't!"

Mr.G said, "Derondon won't."

Coodie moved into the aim of fire, closed his eyes, and Derondon had tears coming down his face. He ran away. Coodie told his classmates nothing happened there. Coodie, Gina, and Menzy ran after Derondon. Derondon disappeared.

The Musketbears headed back to where Derondon may have run off to and Coodie went home to pick up Blue. When they returned home, Blue is gone! Where is Blue? The clouds and winds began to turn more purple and grey! The winds began to sound like screeching laughs of horror similar to amazing actor, Vincent Price!

The Musketbears raced back to the school in search of Mr.G. "Where is Rise?" asked Gina as they raced against the winds. Little did they know, Rise is above them, fighting Romondon and his evil overlord's of destruction! They were tossing objects and creating fear into the minds of apple bears.

They finally made it back to the school. They raced down the hallways, dodging objects. The winds were strong, as a tornado ran rapidly thorough doors and windows. They found Mr. G is sobbing. He is still in the same place when left the last time. "Mr.G, what's going on? Why is the weather looking the way it is?" asked Coodie.

Mr.G, with his hand over his forehead said, "I can't believe one of our bears had gone this far. He has been through a tough life. His mother is coming out of the hospital any day now. Family services are on their way to his home now to take him to jail. What happened in the first place and why did Derondon come back with a weapon?

I told him that he is in the car when it crashed and his seat belt is loose for a reason. Investigators are on the case and his aunt and uncle maybe involved. He got upset and charged me and in the process knocked over a classmate. He aimed his slingshot at the classmate and to distract him I told him he would not amount to anything if he hurt people for the wrong reason.

I know it is wrong to say that and I feel awful. He got angry and pointed his slingshot at me and that's when you came. It is wrong for me to say that to him, but I didn't want to see the innocent bear get hurt," said Mr.G, "Coodie, you can't save everyone."

"Don't give up on him. He's our friend, Mr.G. Everyone has given up on him.

CHAPTER FIFTEEN

We all have a gift from God, Mr.G, even Derondon! Derondon is just begging to find out what it is. He deserves to know so it can guide him to a better life. Will you help us?" asked Coodie.

"Yes!" said Mr.G. Where do you think he went to?" asked Coodie.

"The place of the accident… the park by the lake," said Mr. G. "We know where that is." The Musketbears raced to the park.

"I'm ready to fight," said Menzy said.

"You might get your wish," said Gina. "Well if I fight tomorrow, I'm okay with dat too!"

The Musketbears took a route different from the last time. They discovered a group of bully boys that appeared to guarding a church. It is the back of Coodie's church! Coodie never noticed a door on the side of the church before and it peeked his curiosity even greater. The Musketbears hid behind an abandoned building. "We need a distraction," said Menzy.

"How do you know, Menzy?" asked Gina.

"This is my specialty," said Menzy. "Gina, go out there and pretend to have a heart attack."

"No! Why don't you get a caterpillar and chase them like you did me?" "Ha ha," said Menzy.

"Shhh quiet they will hear us because bully boys are guarding the area. Why don't we do what we did the last time bully boys were on the corner?" said Menzy.

"Follow me and Gina. Go around the side to see what they are guarding and we will meet you back here." "Ok," said Gina.

Menzy got up and Coodie followed his lead. He approached the bully boys. "What's up?" said Menzy.

"Nothing, what are you doing here?"

"We are just coming by to check on everyone. The weather is fierce and so who's guarding you if there is trouble against you?" said Menzy.

"We ahh well..humm I'm not sure. Do you get anything from standing around?" asked Menzy.

"No we are bully boys; we protect our streets and our neighborhood."

"You do," said Menzy. Gina is seen in the background on her toes, checking the backside of the church. In the abandoned building that had lost many logs from the recent winds had an opening. Gina peeked inside and there is Blue tied up! Blue knew Gina. Blue lifted his head to acknowledge Gina. Gina made a gesture of one finger on her mouth for Blue not make a sound. Blue did just that and put his head back down. Just when Menzy nearly convinced that leaving is better than guarding the neighborhood and a house that nobody owned, guess who showed up out of nowhere? If you said Barns, you are right!

The bully boys were about to abandon their post. "And where are you going?" asked Barnes to the bully boys.

"We need to negotiate a contract," said one of the bully boys.

"You boys stay here," said Barns. "So you are trying to turn the boys against me?"

"Barns, take a look around," said Coodie. "Can't you see past you paws! You are a former National ranking Chess Champion! Your winning attitude out performed others amazingly with positive results and recognition!

Winning a tournament in slap-boxing is one thing but taking over the neighborhood we don't own is another thing. That's ugly and why can't someone that looks like you travel to see a friend?

(paces back and forth then to his face to confront)

Why can't someone that has family in your neighborhood travel in this neighborhood and you travel in theirs? How much older do you need to be before you realize there is a big world there and these few streets and boxing tournaments is about as important as giving a whale a peppermint!"

"Are you trying to show how tough you are in front of my friends, Coodie?" said Barns.

"Oooooh Coodie, Barns want to fight you"… slap! "Shhh Menzy," said Gina.

"This is my world down here, Coodie. I run things how I see fit. That is how I put Derondon on you and you didn't know it. Take DAT chess move! He is the one that slapped you, church boy!"

Guess who showed up now? If you said Derondon, then you are right again! Guess who is with him! In the next sentence I promise that the answer is right there!

Derondon came from behind the old building next to the church and Blue is with him. Blue didn't bark because he liked Derondon! Derondon went to find the truth.

He is furious with being confused and angry that nobody had answers to what he is searching for. What happened to his parents? Derondon did have friends and is not prepared to lose friends. He is a Musketbears! Blue saw Coodie and ran to him as Derondon released him.

"Good, Derondon, I'm glad you are here," said Barns,

"Help me check and whip the apple bear cat kids!"

"I am an apple bear cat kid, Barns, don't get it twisted. Checkmate DAT!"

"I knew you were a traitor! I knew it."

"No, Barns, you are the traitor. You are making people believe that protecting something that belongs to us all is yours! You are in your own world trying to prevent what made the neighborhood bleed red… freedom, Barns!"

The police siren increased in its intensity. The police car came with Mr.G and Derondon's parents! They came running to the front of the church. Derondon did something nobody expected him to do, not even you! Derondon walked toward Barns who is steaming angry. Derondon held out his hand to grip a brotherly hug. "I never had a friend before," said Barns and he wept! Bang bang! Went the door from the room that is kept secret!

"Help!" cried a girl's voice.

"I hear a girl's voice," said Gina.

The love of brotherhood woke the princess. "Please open the door; there isn't a handle on my side!" said the princess.

Everyone tried everything to get the door open. "Who are you?"

"Is that Coodie talking?" said the princess. "I know who you are. You have a large heart! I've been watching you in my dreams! Find my brother. He will know what to do."

The winds had not died down and are getting worse. Barns agreed to help and the Musketbears that has grown to five! The clouds were not only thicker but darker and people were attacking each other.

Rise fought with might and will. A ton of negative pulse is relentless and applied his senses including sight, fought through pulses, removed the energy from the sky and hearts of people to prevent the negative energy from growing any stronger. Out of the skies came Romondon and his power grew at a rate that Rise had never faced before.

With a mighty pulse of negative energy, Rise became blinded by the wavy pulse of purple and grey light that blinded his vision causing him to fly into a state confusion and into a bell that cracked and knocked him unconscious.

Coodie looked into the ceiling of the church. He is beginning to lose what he all of what he is made of. Faith is seeping from his mind. He appeared visibly shaky. His eyes of hope made their way to a reflection in the stained glass of the church! Rise, above, continued fighting the pulses of negative spells that shot from the clouds beyond the surface of the skies. Coodie thought about a feeling he experienced when he is in the car riding and commenting on the very substance of light and when he asked his mother about the reflection of stained glass on the various churches. His friends asked him why he is staring at the stained glass windows.

Coodie stated with a low volume and voice, "There is something about religion, I don't understand but I got it!" It hit Coodie! Coodie ran out of the church and raced to the center of Bearsville. Coodie, Gina, and Menzy followed. Derondon stood in the doorway and beyond him is a pack of bully boys!

The bully boys began to surround Coodie, Menzy, and Gina. Coodie stepped forward and before he could utter a word. A team of bully boys attacked him. The fight is witnessed through the eyes of Menzy. His reaction told the story and fight scene.

"I told you, Coodie is fast and quick!" "Look. .oooo duck oohh… who… he, he," the shadows and reflections of bully-bears flying left and right! The Musketbears fought their way out and into the streets! Coodie promised himself to get help for the princess.

Chapter Sixteen (final Chapter)

Coodie's determination is visible as he maintained his focus by reading signs on widows of light-green from various churches. Bears everywhere were following their minds and ignoring their hearts. One by one, aggression, arguing, and fighting!

"Somehow we lost our way!" Coodie yelled. Coodie and the four Musketbear darted down the street, hearing sirens, screams, crying, fights, car accidents, and more fights!

"What were your childhood dreams?" Coodie screamed and so did the others Musketbears! "You are heroes!" You are misguided by ugliness! It must not take over your minds! Hold on to what is dear to you your child."

Make your God proud of you! Barns' eyes began to see for himself. His eyes began to fill with water. Barns said, "Nobody has ever made me take a look at my heart before and remember my childhood dreams!... "I am a hero and my heart is happy." Barns moved close to Coodie and said, "How can I be a hero again?"

Coodie replied, "The instant you show kindness!"

Barns began to open the doors of the Churches they walked through and told Coodie, Gina, and Menzy.

"Please allow me, after you, please, thank you too, and with honor, have an amazing day!"

Derondon, Gina and Menzy followed him. Gina and Menzy asked what it is. Coodie said he didn't know but to follow him. Coodie felt if he could be heard by many then maybe they would listen answered will discover their gift. The three needed a place where they could be heard. There is a basketball game and it is nearly halftime.

Romondon completely forgot about buildings that sealed off from sound and sight—the Spectrum in Philadelphia. Home of the Spirits of Philadelphia and Brotherly Love! Coodie, Gina, and Menzy slipped through the guards, posing as security guards. They made their way to the Spectrum's floor.

At half time, the show is about to start. Right before the band members were about to walk to their set, Coodie took the mic, Menzy took the drum set, and Gina took the guitar. The original band thought the act is part of the show. The guards that noticed that their jackets were taken away went searching for the crew they seen last. Coodie, Gina, and Menzy! Coodie told Menzy and Gina to play a melody. Derondon went inside the control room, making recordings to broadcast to satellites across the world. The crowd is excited, hungry, and curious at the same time. The announcers at the booth asked if this is part of the show. The management at the top listened to the reaction of the crowd began to cheer and become enthusiastic.

They began to clap at a pace to set a rhythm before a note is played. The claps and stumps also came to play. Coodie took the mic and sang along the phrase, "Something about religion I don't understand but I got it!" The rhythm and beat slowly formed. The original band members began to join in.

Coodie listened to his own words with his heart. He struggled to find the words from the song that ended with a note, a key sound, a missing ingredient that touched the hearts of church members everywhere. The cheers, stomps, and claps of support increased.

"Coodie, what's wrong? You are not singing." "What should we do?" asked Gina.

"Just keep singing," said Menzy "right, Coodie?" The chorus that Coodie initiated is all he could remember.

Derondon did it! He managed to make contact with everyone all over the world. Derondon remembered Coodie's affection for magnets. He took a magnet from under the microphone stand and tied it to the back of several cameras locked the signal and pointed it to a satellite in space and it worked! The fans and Musketbears cheered on Derondon's ingenuity. He is connected to every reception possible within media. Derondon attended Coodie's church and he realized the missing ingredient!

Derondon hopped over to the announcer's box, took the mic and began to chant, "Rise, Rise, Rise, Rise, Rise!"

Coodie witness his angel, Rise in action ABOVE! Rise is 2000 times his size defending Coodie from Romondon! In Coodie's eyes reveals an overwhelming feeling that generates appreciation that united church and community connecting inward and influences outwardly spiritually! The rhythm reached the height of the chorus, Coodie let out an amazing sound that set the crowd into a frenzy! An enormous eruption of love and beautiful spirit filled the Spectrum! Overhead through the ceiling is Rise seen by Coodie as a giant! Coodie lifts his head to Rise! To his surprise, Coodie erupts!

"YAHEEE YAHEEE YAHEEE YAHHHHH! YAHEEE YAHEEE YAHEEE YAHHHHH!" CLEARING UP LIGHT GREEN!!"

Romondon's speed of pulse energy to travel is reduced to a slower rate.

"Foils! My POWERS has weakened! I'm reduced to the thought of those Apple Bears singing! This must STOP!"

He checked his coordinates and flew to the spectrum.

"He must be stopped!"

At the church Rise's visibility and size gets reversed from loss of energy momentarily! On his back beaten and drained in and out of awareness Rise sees ducks playing with cats and children playing with their dog. The animals are coexisting in friendship. He turns his head to overhear the event of Coodie, Gina, and Menzy singing on the television set! Unaware that the princess is locked in a room near him, Rise Rose to the sound of Juan-Tracy's voice of confidence! Rise's energy began to fill his heart from the clouds above showing the color light-green! The energy of light green allowed him to absorb instantly as he's connected in spirit.

RISE
His glasses flashes!
"The-Apple-Bears-need-your-help!"
Rise rose! His walk turned into a trout then into a
run then into flight!
Juan-Tracy
Rise are you there!
The Apple Bears need you!
Rise (acknowledges) I'm dialed in!
Juan-tracy
Welcome back Rise I'm thrilled to know you are
revitalized! Romondon is heading to the Spectrum
as we speak! His powers has weakened thanks to the
Apple Bears!

At the Spectrum kindness roamed again inside
the Spectrum and its broadcast made its way to
televisions sets and animals around the world. Reads;
"Let not your heart be troubled!" Heroes came
forward that roamed the airwaves to tell amazing
stories of others, themselves, and the ugliness
for attention became insufficient as it raced like
tickertape during the bottom of the screens! Coodie,
the musketeer's began to dance and bears that
watched the dance began to follow. Joy, love, kindness,
and peace are important again and it mattered! Rise
flew over the Spectrum. Rise's heart doubled in size!

Rise's energy returns and reaches the source, his best friend the princess. Enormous energy raced to him as evident of vibrant green causes him to luminous light!

"Let not your heart be troubled! Indeed!" said Rise from his reflection of the bible.

Romondon flew inside the spectrum but it is empty. It's a recording coming from the speaker system! Coodie, Menzy, and Gina hid in the studio! Romondon hid inside the purple cloud to avoid being seen. He is unaware of an odor within the intensity of his anger. He moves closer to investigate! He sees the Musketbears as they are unaware of the mirror of their reflection coming from a dull metal panel! It reveals movement. Romondon's confidence reveals his face as he aims his ring and sends a spell in the direction of the Musketbears. His odor triggers Coodie's thought of the janitor that gave him the mint candy. Coodie is shocked!

"Yahhee-Yahhee-Yehhee, YAHHHH!-Yikes!
His mouth is quickly covered by Menzy and Gina! Shhhhh…

In the process the mint fell from his pocket!

Coodie reaches in his pocket for the mint to return a favor! The mint is gone! He lowers his head in disappointment and turns away to hide. In the process he can see Romondon aiming his ring in the grey panel. Menzy, unaware that Romondon can see them. Owe!! Coodie did you fart! What is DAT smell? Derondon gestures at Menzy with one finger over his mouth followed by making a fist over his eye followed by his other eye then his mouth for Menzy to quiet down! Derondon finished with a smile then moved his mouth to say,

"Thank you!"

Barns' eyes react to Derondon's non-verbal and reacts with a mean face for Menzy to focus. He nods in approval and in the process, his eyes reads Coodie's disappointment to find the mint candy. He locates the mint candy lying near Coodie and just out of reach. He points and whispers!

"PSSST! Oh-Look!"

Coodie reaches for the mint! The motion slows as Romondon points his ring and spews his spell-casting words of destruction!

The vibration of the panel that is attached to the heavy speaker begins to reverberate into the Musketbears direction!

"Once and for all! And all for one for no more! Bu-sud-Besiddo!"

As Romondon yells his words to force the speaker to destroy the Musketbears, Coodie is unaware he's seen extending his hand with the final attempt he is successful with his reach. He comes to his feet turns to face Romondon, he tosses with all his might at Romondon's mouth. With success he tosses the mint that is laced with sleeping potion inside Romondon's mouth before he could complete the casting spell and that unleashes power from his ring! His voice is blocked by the mint candy that grew in size while in route to his tonsil. He chokes!

"AURRRGH!"

The mint begins to rapidly take its effect on Romondon's swallow!

CRASH!

Crash went the roof of the spectrum! The roof that is made of glass and metal slams the floor as Rise flew into Romondon. Romondon caught Rise and tossed him like a rag doll.

Rise fought with all he had but Romondon is far too strong. Rise never gave up as each opportunity to slip a punch or duck a kick allow him to contract when Romondon expended and when Romondon contracted Rise expanded. Rise used his speed against power and stayed a distance until he is ready to throw a blow.

Outside shows birds in parks are playing with the squirrels and at zoo the lions are playing with the zebras forcing more power of green that generates

Rise's power. People all around began to see how animals were examples of love and kindness. The effects of positivity energized earth's core and it's gravitational pull expanded its path of love resulting in God's intentions of harmony and reason. Handshakes, hugs, apologies, opening doors for others increased!

Rise flashes a reflection on his protective shield to the Land of Reason!

On the land of Reason the birds and other animals made their way from untouched sections of their planet to sing, play, and show love and affection toward the people. They sent them to aid Rise with weakening Romondon's wrath. The energy on earth had made it way to the church.

Rise grew stronger and Romondon's power decreased and left him with ordinary magical powers! Rise and Romondon erupted with power at each blow. Rise reflected to the words of the princess.

"It is the eyes of intelligence that, (gasps for air!) that. …"

Rise began to tilt his head to remove his mask. He is in full force with all senses at full throttle.

THAT..

"My eyes that assist me increases my accuracy of delivery!"

Rise frees himself with a burst of energy onto his suit! Romondon failed with every magical strike. Romondon is defenseless. Rise threw thunder bolts and struck Romondon in the heart and he exploded! The contact is great enough to open the eyes and the impact that release of the spell on the door of the princess and the king's heart! The princess, the queen's daughter appeared before her mother by her bedside. The queen lying still hasn't opened her eyes! Princess saw her mother the queen in her dreams! Her connection with her mother and father the king is amazing! The light of the land of Reason glows because of love for modeling the castle to look just like its kingdom! The essence, purpose, reason, growth, and power that visibly shines in the hearts of people derives from the king, queen, prince and princess energy.

PRINCESS KAHLIA

Mother I remember everything you taught me. I remember how you taught me how to garden fruits, and vegetables. You kept the gates open to create trust among our people. You, me, Rise, and father held hands as we walked into town to the market to talk, share,..share seeds and pottery ideas as well as dig the dirt to grow fruits and vegetables just like ours. You showed me how to be proud, peaceful and polite with kindness and with stories of how you met father to make children safe and discover their gifts carries a glow inside me and out. I love you mother for making me who I am and the Land of Reason is thankful for us modeling excellence. I need you, will you return to us… mother,… will you return..return to us…

A tear began to roll out of the queen's eye onto the pillow that lands on the hand of the princess! The Queen's face that once remained still showed life with color and movement. The king made his way inside the doorway of the entrance of the castle, rushed up the stairs to the entrance of the bedroom to hear his daughter the princess restate with her head down holding her mother's hand by the bedside. Mother will you return to us.. Princess Kahlia's heart and body had a glow that shined bright enough to fill the room! Light began to flow from the lining of each window, door, structure of the castle and gate!

My Queen!

The Queen opened her eyes! The glow of the Princess indicated love and key to kindness. The princess became startled by the appearance of the King's comment. She held her head up felt the warmth of her mother's hand and turned to her mother the Queen has returned to her! –

A glorious day! Indeed!

The princess kissed her mother, cries joyful tears and placed her head on her mother's bosom.

"I love you mother!"

LAND OF REASON OUTSIDE THE CASTLE KING DONTAVIUS,

"A glorious day! A glorious day indeed! Thank God for this glorious day!

QUEEN,

"I'm sorry I was away! I love you all and our kingdom! Please tell me where is our son Rise?"

THROUGH THE TUNNEL TO THE LAND OF REASON

Rise is sent through as he fought off the blast of energy that sent him back to the Land of Reason!

"Nooooo! Not without my sister! Nooooooo!"

He managed to turn his body against the blast!

"I can't return without my sister! Noooooo!"

ON THE LAND OF REASON OUTSIDE THE CASTLE NEAR AN OAK TREE!

At the point of exhaustion, bewilderment, restlessness, concerned, and fearfulness of returning to the Land of Reason without his sister. Rise lands in a kneeled position. He comes to his feet out of extreme hesitation, his head is last to come up. He knows his father will be the first face he sees! Rise feeling he failed after all he could do is look to the ground and back with his shoulder's slumped to utter his last amount of words of hope. His father the King is waiting on his arrival just like he thought. Tears begin to fill his protective face shield. Each step brings a level of sadness and loss. His father the king sees Rise, walks toward him upon his landing, and greets him with his hands and arms in an opened position to embrace him. The King know that his son Rise loves his sister dearly, recognizes Rise's sadness and feeling that he failed delivers a fatherly approach to reassure he in-fact saved his friend and sister's return to the Land of Reason safely and saved both worlds!

Rise feels a sense of loss of all he has learned and have been taught that is pure from kindness. Each step shortens to hear the worse news he could ever hear. Is the princess, my friend, my sister safe?

KING DONTAVIUS

"Yes, she is safe and on her way to see you!"

Rise began to cry, thinking he lost his best friend, the princess.

Rise (protective wear filled with tears-struggles to make eye contact)

"I'm sorry I failed you."

KING DONTAVIUS,

"You haven't failed."

(as the princess came to Rise to kiss him on the cheek.)

PRINCESS KAHLIA

(behind him smiling, and listening, her familiar voice rang amazement to Rise's ears!)

"You are a hero and you kept the movement alive and well. (kiss..) But it was kindness that saved us!"

Rise's tears became tears of joy. Juan-Tracy sat on a branch above!

JUAN-TRACY,

"Yeah! Great job best friend! Great job!"

Rise turned to see that Juan-

Tracy is speaking with his voice.

Juan-Tracy

"Whaaaaaatt".…. (softly)

LAND OF REASON OUTSIDE THE CASTLE

KING DONTAVIUS,

"A glorious day! A glorious day indeed! Thank God for this glorious day!

RISE,

(Joyful tears) "Fantastic Juan-Tracy! You're talking!"

"An honor and a blessing! Indeed!"

The animals came out of the woods to great the people.

JUAN-TRACY,

"Life of light and energy returned to the woods
and lands everywhere!" (Hops down from the branch)
"I fell into the loving arms of God!"
Slow winds from the tunnel in a distance!
"Rise, Rise, Rise! Rise! Rise!"
RISE,
"Who is calling me?" (walks toward the tunnel)
KING, QUEEN, AND KAHLIA
"Let's go look."
They could hear Coodie with his mother, his
family, the Musketbears, media, and the entire world
as one saying his name at the same time!
RISE!!
Is it me whom they are requesting?

The end!.....
Or is it?

I observed things like nature and how well birds and other animals work together. I observed the behavior of animals and discovered that they are nice to each other. I observed that nature is God's way of showing what working together looks like. I like how it made me feel.

I kept my focus on nature and allowed its messages to send. My affinity to attach myself to nature through observation, imagination and traded places with birds, butterflies, grasshoppers, and bees that buffered my sadness. In spite of how much anger that went on all over the place, I kept God in my heart and kept my focus! I made it a habit to observe and not be quick to speak on life's hard lessons and abuse. As the scars of anger plagued my family and its affects as it tricked down to me as the youngest of five, I learned to be a grasshopper for survival. I was too young to understand so I kept my focus! Just like the bee that learned to go around an object that disrupts its path, I studied and simply moved on, I kept my focus! And so can you!